夫子如在

——曲阜孔庙公祭孔子大典祭文注译（2004—2023）

CONFUCIUS SEEMS TO BE PRESENT

Qufu Confucius Temple Confucius Commemoration Ceremony
Text Annotation and Translation (From 2004 to 2023)

白占德　李　芳　主编

中国文史出版社
CHINA CULTURAL AND HISTORICAL PRESS

图书在版编目（CIP）数据

夫子如在 : 曲阜孔庙公祭孔子大典祭文注译 : 2004—
2023 / 白占德 , 李芳主编 . -- 北京 : 中国文史出版社 ,
2024. 5. -- ISBN 978-7-5205-4715-4

Ⅰ . K892.98

中国国家版本馆 CIP 数据核字第 2024Z61H11 号

责任编辑：刘华夏
装帧设计：艾永久　　王晓雨

出版发行：中国文史出版社
社　　址：北京市海淀区西八里庄路 69 号　邮编：100142
电　　话：010-81136606 / 6602 / 6603 / 6642（发行部）
传　　真：010-81136655
印　　装：山东成信彩印有限公司　0537-2379999
经　　销：全国新华书店
开　　本：710mm×1000mm　1/16
字　　数：200 千字
印　　张：19.5
版　　次：2024 年 9 月北京第 1 版
印　　次：2024 年 9 月第 1 次印刷
定　　价：88.00 元

序

　　读懂孔庙，才能读懂中国。每每谈到孔庙、说到祭孔，我就很自然想说这样的话。孔子以后的2000多年中，孔子祭祀关涉信仰与道德的传承，文庙祭祀系统在中国文化传承体系中居于特殊的重要地位。

　　中国是礼仪之邦，向来重视礼仪活动，祭祀则是其中最重要的方面，所以古时有"国之大事，在祀与戎""礼有五经，莫重于祭"的说法。《周礼》还有"以祀礼教敬"之说，祭祀之礼用以培养人们的敬畏之心。比如，古人会祭祀天地，祭祀人鬼，这都是为了表示敬畏和敬重。祭祀孔子，其实代表了我们对于以孔子为代表的中华传统文化的尊重与礼敬。

　　孔庙本称为"文庙"，因为主祭孔子而被简称。在世界众多祭祀孔子的庙堂中，孔子故里曲阜的孔庙规模最大、历史最久。唐代以后，各府州县皆立孔庙，孔庙数量越来越多。纵观历朝历代，俯视寰宇九州，虽然不少世代都是"天下名山僧占尽"，佛寺、道观乃至其他庙宇也恢宏壮丽，夺人眼目，然而，与佛寺、道观多在山中、云端不同，孔庙作为传统中国的文庙，都位于人们聚居之地。随着时代的变化，孔庙教化社会的功能日渐凸显，孔子儒学渐渐走进中国人的内心世界，孔子的地位也变得崇高起来。

孔庙祭祀典礼又称"释奠礼"。孔子去世后，民间就开始了对他的祭祀。官方祭祀孔子则始于汉初，汉高祖十二年，刘邦自淮南过鲁，以太牢祀孔子，开历代帝王祭孔之先河。东汉明帝时期，修明养老习射之礼，郡县道学校皆祭祀周公孔子，于是孔子始祀于庠序之间。唐玄宗册封孔子为"文宣王"，祭祀规格跨上极高的等级，经明、清乃至民国，孔庙祭祀越来越盛。

孔庙主祭孔子，而以四配、十二哲配享，大成殿的两庑还有150多名先贤、先儒从祀。如果说孔子所确立和阐述的价值观念是中国人的立足点，那么，在孔庙中配享、从祀孔子的人物，则是这些价值观的践行者、弘扬者、光大者。要知道，从唐代以来，谁来配享、从祀孔子，都是官方议定的，这些配祀孔子的人是历代的大儒。可以说，孔子以及那些配享、从祀孔子的人，正是中国的脊梁。孔庙作为中国的文庙，是传统中国的"名人堂"或"先贤祠"，是传统中国知识分子的精神家园。

由于历史的原因，民国以来孔庙祭祀曾经有半个多世纪的沉寂，1984年始，曲阜开展了孔子故里游活动，孔庙开始再现祭孔仪式。此后，在历届孔子文化节中，祭孔大典都备受瞩目。2004年，祭孔大典改由官方公办，祭祀规格得到质的提高。2005年全球联合祭孔，2006年"同根一脉，两岸祭孔"，2007年全球华人华侨祭孔等，都产生了良好的社会影响，祭孔大典也被列入首批国家级非物质文化遗产名录。2013 年 11 月 26 日，习近平总书记考察孔子故里曲阜，在孔子研究院举行专家学者座谈会；2014 年 9 月 24 日，习近平总书记在北京出席纪念孔子诞辰 2565 周年大会并发表讲话，对孔子的纪念上升到国家最高层面。最近 10 年来，传统文化弘扬更加深入展开，祭孔大典越来越受到人们的重视，每年的孔子文化节期间，孔庙祭祀也是备受世界瞩目的"大典"。

在历届释奠礼中，祭文又成为整个礼典的灵魂或者核心。20 年来，我十分幸运也感到光荣之至，自己不仅撰写了 2011 年的祭文，而且曲阜公祭孔子的第一年，我就很荣幸地参与了撰写祭文的讨论，此后几乎每年都是祭文的第一读者。济宁市领导注意发挥学者们的作用，每年祭文初稿出来之后，都要邀请省内高校、研究机构有关学者组成专家组，进行研析论证，我近水楼台，总能最早得以拜读学习。作为曾经恭撰祭文的人，我更理解每一位作者，相信大家都会倾注情感，严肃对待，认真思考，全力以赴。祭文代表了作者对传统文化的敬重，表达了对孔子思想价值的认识，体现了对孔子思想精髓的理解。

夫子如在，孔子和历代圣哲的精神与中华民族同在，孔子确立与阐述的价值观念历代传承，使中华民族和谐和平地共同生活了几千年。传统中国以"神道设教"，这是一种人文文化。"祭如在，祭神如神在"，在祭祀典礼中，在乐舞洋洋中，在祭文诵读中，人们与孔子和圣哲心灵相遇、精神相通。

本书共汇聚 2004 年以来的祭文 20 篇，这些作品粲然成章，风格各异。细细读来，或比兴铺排，言辞对仗；或立意高远，气象非凡；或溯古追今，娓娓道来；或依经据典，发微古意。可以说，这都是上乘的文学作品，也是珍贵的文化遗产。祭文皆为文言文形式，言辞古奥，现代人理解起来有一定困难。因此，济宁市文化传承发展中心组织力量，汇集20篇祭文，并加以注释、现代文翻译和英译，成书《夫子如在》一书。初读其中译文，感觉文通句顺，言近旨远，风格清丽而不失庄严。祭文得以文白对照、中英对读，可以让更多的人都能品味其中悠长的文化意涵。对于宣传祭孔大典，弘扬孔子儒学思想，这是一个重要贡献！

是为序！

2024年3月22日于曲阜圣水苑

Foreword

Understanding the Confucian Temple is a unique way to understand China. Whenever I talk about the Confucian Temple or mention the worship of Confucius, such words naturally come to my mind. For over 2,000 years, the worship of Confucius has been involved in the inheritance of faith and morality, and the system of honoring Confucius occupies a special and important position in the Chinese cultural inheritance system.

China is a nation of ritual and righteousness, always valuing ceremonial activities, with worship activities being the most important aspect. Therefore, there are some Chinese sayings from ancient times called "The great affairs of the country are in worship and military," and "Among the five classics of rituals, nothing is more important than worship." "The Book of Rites" also states, "Using ritual sacrifice to teach reverence," indicating that the rituals of worship are used to cultivate people's sense of awe. For instance, in ancient times, people would worship heaven and earth, and worship ancestors and spirits, all to show reverence and respect. Similarly, commemorating Confucius actually represents our respect and reverence for the excellent traditional Chinese culture represented by Confucianism.

The Confucian Temple, originally called the "Temple of Literature," is abbreviated because of Confucius worship. Among those many temples worshiping Confucius all around the world, the Confucian

Temple in Qufu, where Confucius was born, is the largest in scale and the longest in history. Since the Tang Dynasty, temples dedicated to Confucius have been established in various prefectures, counties, and townships, and the number of Confucian temples has been increasing gradually with dynasty replacement. Throughout a long history, many generations were building popular Buddhist and Taoist temples in famous mountains, which are so grand and magnificent that they captur people's attention. However, unlike Buddhist temples and Taoist temples mostly located in the mountains, Confucian temples, as traditional Chinese literary temples, are located where people gather. With the change of the times, the function of educating society in Confucian temples has become increasingly prominent. Confucianism has gradually entered the inner world of the Chinese people, and the status Confucius has also become elevated.

The ceremony of honoring Confucius in the Confucian Temple is also called "The Rite of Release and Offering." folk worship of Confucius began after his death. Official worship of Confucius began in the early Han Dynasty. In the twelfth year of Emperor Gaozu of Han, Emperor Liu Bang passed by Lu area from Huainan area and sacrificed to Confucius with a great offering, setting a precedent for emperors and kings to worship Confucius in later generations. During the Eastern Han Dynasty, the rituals of elderly providing and archery training were performed. Therefore, Confucius was commonly worshipped in the schools of prefectures and counties, which is the beginning of honoring Confucius between the hall of learning and the hall of court ceremony. Emperor Xuanzong of the Tang Dynasty conferred the title of "Wenxuan King" on Confucius, and the standard of the worship increased significantly. Since the

Ming and Qing Dynasties, and even the Republic of China, the worship of Confucius has become increasingly grand.

The Confucian Temple primarily worships Confucius, with offerings made to four sages and twelve philosophers, as well as more than 150 other scholars and philosophers along both side of Dacheng Hall. If the value system established and elucidated by Confucius is the foundation of the Chinese people, in that way, those who are worshipped and revered with Confucius in the Confucian Temple are the practitioners, promoters, and magnifiers of these values. It should be noted that since the Tang Dynasty, the people who have been worshipped and would be worshipped with Confucius have been determined by central government, and all of these people are great scholars and philosophers of each generation. It can be said that Confucius and those worshipped with Confucius are the backbone of China. As the literary temple of China, Confucian Temples can also be nominated as the "hall of fame" or "temple of sages" of traditional China. It is the permanent spiritual home of traditional Chinese intellectuals.

Due to historical reasons, there was no worship in the Confucian Temple for more than half a century since the Republic of China era. In 1984, Qufu launched an event called the Confucius's Hometown Tour, which had a brand new name of China International Confucius Culture Festival in 1989, and Qufu Confucian Temple began to revive the ceremony of worshiping Confucius. From then on, in annual China International Confucius Cultural Festival, the ceremony has been commonly focused and anticipated. In 2004, the worship ceremony was officially organized by the government, and the standards of the ceremony were greatly elevated. In 2005, the Global

United Confucius Commemoration was held, followed by events like "Roots Shared, Joint Commemoration of Confucius across Taiwan Straits" in 2006 and "the United Commemoration of Confucius by Global Chinese Descendants" in 2007, all of which made positive social impact. The commemoration ceremony of Confucius was also listed as one of the first items of national intangible cultural heritage. On November 26th, 2013, General Secretary of the Central Committee of the Communist Party of China, Xi Jinping, visited the hometown of Confucius, Qufu, and held a symposium with experts and scholars at the Confucius Research Institute. On September 24th, 2014, General Secretary Xi Jinping attended the commemoration of the 2,565th anniversary of Confucius' birth in Beijing and delivered a speech, elevating the commemoration of Confucius to the highest national level. During the past decade, the promotion of excellent traditional culture has become more widespread, and the worship ceremonies of Confucius have received increasing attention. In every Confucius Cultural Festival, the Commemoration Ceremony at Qufu Confucian Temple has become a highly anticipated event worldwide. In the previous ceremonies, the text of commemoration has become the soul or essence of the entire ritual. Over the past twenty years, I have felt incredibly fortunate and honored to write the text in 2011, and also privileged to participate in the discussions on drafting the text in the first year of commemoration. Almost every year thereafter, I have been among the first readers of the commemoration text. The municipal leaders of Jining have recognized the role of scholars, inviting experts from universities and research institutions within and outside of Shandong province to form expert panels for analysis and discussion when the initial draft of the commemoration text is completed annually. Being close to the source, I have always had the earliest opportunity to study and learn these famous articles. As someone who has once composed commemoration texts, I understand each author's sentiments, believing that everyone dedicates their emotions, treats the task seriously, considers deeply, and devotes their full effort to make it excellent. The commemoration text represents the authors' reverence for traditional culture, expresses their understanding of the value of Confucian thoughts, and embodies their comprehension of the essence of Confucian philosophy.

The spirit of Confucius and the sages of past generations resonate with the entire Chinese nation, perpetuating the values established and elucidated by Confucius throughout history, enabling the Chinese nation to live together in harmony and peace for thousands of years. Traditional China follows the concept of "establishing education through reverence for the divine," which embodies a humanistic culture. "In the ceremony, Confucius is present." During the commemoration ceremony, enjoying the elegant music and dance, and in the recitation of sacrificial texts, people encounter the spirits of Confucius and the sages, establishing a spiritual connection.

This book gathers a total of 20 commemoration texts since 2004, all of them are well-crafted and exhibit diverse styles. Upon close examination, they feature elaborate metaphors, balanced expressions, lofty aspirations, extraordinary imagery, historical retrospections, and classical allusions. It can be said that these are all superior literary works and valuable cultural heritage. These texts are all in classical Chinese language, making them difficult for modern readers to read and understand. Therefore, Jining Municipal Cultural Inheritance and Development Center made great efforts to compile these texts, providing annotations, modern Chinese translations, and English translations in the book. Upon initial reading of these annotated and translated texts, people can feel its clarity, fluency, and graceful style while maintaining dignity. With the commemoration texts presented bilingually in both Chinese and English, more people can appreciate the profound cultural significance inside. These efforts contribute significantly to promoting Confucius Commemoration Ceremony and spreading the essence of Confucianism, which is a crucial contribution!

With utmost respect, I present passage above as the preface of this book.

Yang Chaoming

March 22nd, 2024, at Shengshuiyuan, Qufu

前 言

"一个国家、一个民族的强盛，总是以文化兴盛为支撑的，中华民族伟大复兴需要以中华文化发展繁荣为条件。"2013年11月，习近平总书记视察济宁，发出大力弘扬中华优秀传统文化的号召。

济宁是中华文明重要发祥地，是儒家文化发源地，文化传承发展使命光荣。全市干部群众牢记嘱托，深入践行习近平文化思想，在文化"两创"中不断展现新作为，为建设中华民族现代文明贡献了济宁力量。特别是近年来，在济宁市委、市政府的坚强领导下，连续成功举办中国国际孔子文化节、尼山世界文明论坛等一系列具有国际影响力的大型文化活动，大大加快了全国一流文化名市、世界文化旅游名城的建设步伐。

中国国际孔子文化节是当代文化活动的高山，被称为"国之大典"的祭孔大典是这座高山的主峰。2500多年来的祭孔活动中，祭文作为这座文化主峰的顶点，发挥着不可替代的核心作用。在国内诸多祭祀活动中，济宁市首开"邀请权威专家、国学大师撰写祭文"先河。2004年恢复公祭孔子大典以来的20

篇祭文，凝聚着金庸、范曾、许嘉璐、张立文等大家学者的情感和心血，发古意承述千年文脉，述新风启迪辉煌征程，洋洋洒洒、斐然成章。这些祭文佳作，已然成为孔子思想和儒家文化的宝贵遗产，必将传诵后世，流芳万年。

祭文均为赋体，言辞古奥，用典繁多。为帮助更多中外专家学者和文化爱好者进一步理解祭文内涵，扩大儒学国际交流传播，向世界讲好中国故事和济宁故事，市文化传承发展中心组织力量，历时数月完成了20篇祭文的注释、现代文翻译和英文翻译，成书《夫子如在——曲阜孔庙公祭孔子大典祭文注译（2004—2023）》，由中国文史出版社出版。

今年是孔子诞辰2575年，是逢五举办纪念孔子活动的"大年"，全国和世界各地都将隆重举办纪念孔子的系列活动。伴随《夫子如在》的出版，孔子故里正式开启纪念活动的新篇章。展望未来，济宁将自觉以文化传承发展为使命，推动以儒家文化为代表的中华优秀传统文化更好地走向世界，在建设中华民族现代文明的实践中展现新作为、彰显新担当。

济宁市文化传承发展中心

2024 年 3 月

Preface

"A nation's prosperity and strength always rely on the flourishing of its culture. The great rejuvenation of the Chinese nation requires the development and prosperity of Chinese culture as its foundation". In November 2013, General Secretary of the Central Committee of the Communist Party of China, Xi Jinping inspected Jining and called for vigorously promoting the excellent traditional Chinese culture.

Jining is an important origin of Chinese civilization and the birthplace of Confucian culture, with the glorious mission of culture inheritance and development. Cadres and masses throughout the city have kept this instruction in mind, deeply implementing the Cultural policies advocated by Xi Jinping , continuously demonstrating new achievements in cultural innovation and creation, and contributing Jining's strength to modern Chinese civilization. Especially in recent years, under the strong leadership of the Jining Municipal Party Committee and Government, a series of large-scale cultural events with international influence, such as the China International Confucius Culture Festival and the Nishan World Civilization Forum, have been successfully held, greatly accelerating the pace of constructing a first-class cultural city in China and a world-renowned cultural and tourist city.

The China International Confucius Culture Festival is a pinnacle of current cultural activities, acclaimed as "the Grand Ceremony of the Nation", the and Confucius Commemoration Ceremony is a peak of this mountain. For over 2,500 years, commemoration texts have played an irreplaceable core role in the Confucius memorial activities. Among numerous domestic memorial ceremonies, Jining City pioneered the practice of inviting authoritative experts and masters of Chinese studies to write commemoration texts. In 2004, the Confucius Commemoration Ceremony in Qufu Confucius Temple resumed; since then, 20 commemoration texts have been condensed with great emotional efforts and contributions of distinguished figures such as Louis Cha Leung-yung, Fan Zeng, Xu Jialu, and Zhang Liwen. They inherited the ancient essence and illuminated the brilliant journey of enlightenment with new ideas, written eloquently and profoundly. These excellent commemoration texts have become precious heritages of Confucian thoughts and culture, destined to be passed down through generations and remain eternal.

The commemoration texts are all written in a poetic style, with profound language and various allusions. In order to help more Chinese and foreign experts, researchers, and cultural enthusiasts further understand the connotations of the commemoration texts, and tell China's and Jining's stories to the world via expanding international communication and dissemination of Confucianism, Jining Municipal Cultural Inheritance and Development Center put great efforts and spent several months completing annotations, modern Chinese translations, and English translations for these 20 commemoration texts, with the title of "Confucius Seems to Be Present: Qufu Confucius Temple Confucius Commemoration Ceremony Text Annotation and Translation (From 2024 to 2023)." It is published by China Cultural and Historical Press.

This year marks the 2575th anniversary of Confucius's birth, a significant milestone known as a "Grand Year" in every five years. There will be a series of domestic and global memorial activities for honoring Confucius. With the publication of "Confucius Seems to Be Present," Confucius's hometown officially initiates a new chapter in its commemoration activities. Looking forward, Jining will shoulder the mission of cultural inheritance and development, promoting the dissemination of excellent traditional Chinese culture, represented by Confucianism, to the world. In the practice of building the modern Chinese civilization, Jining will demonstrate new achievements and show new responsibilities.

Jining Municipal Cultural Inheritance and Development Center

March 2024

目录

Catalogue

2004 甲申年

纪念先哲　承扬文化
促进开放　创新发展

2004, the Jiashen Year.
Commemorating our ancestors, promoting culture, fostering openness, and innovating development.

纪念孔子诞辰

2555

年

Commemorating the 2555th Anniversary of Confucius's Birth

甲申（2004）年祭孔大典祭文

杨佐仁　撰

维公元 2004 年 9 月 28 日，岁在甲申，节届中秋，先师孔子诞辰 2555 年，曲阜各界代表、海内外宾朋、孔子后裔，肃立大成殿前，谨以鲜花雅乐，恭祭先师孔子。文曰：

文圣吾祖，恩泽海宇。千古巨人，万世先师。

欣逢盛世，物阜民熙[1]。高岸秀木，惟恐失序。

居安思危[2]，重振纲纪[3]。以德治国，德法兼济[4]。

幸赖圣儒，万代垂仪。道贯古今，德侔天地。

杏坛春晖[5]，泮池桃李[6]。三坟五典[7]，六经[8]古籍。

薪火传承，百代不熄。而今吾辈，见贤思齐[9]。

任重道远，弘扬承继。依仁志道，据德游艺[10]。

仁为己任，见利思义[11]。中和至德，过犹不及。

和协万邦，摒弃暴戾。刚健[12]有为，自强不息[13]。

与时偕进，创新活力。清风遍拂，神州万里。

群情振奋，勃发骐骥。文化名城，通衢[14]如砥。

碧树花团，芬苾争奇。百业兴隆，日新月异。

近悦远来 [15]，治平修齐。老养壮用 [16]，兆民 [17] 甘饴。

儒风犹在，先圣故里。慎终追远，奋吾国膂。

继往开来，同德凝聚。东方巨龙，吼啸腾起。

四海擎天，有吾一臂。长鲸吞吐，丹凤鼓翼。

揽月追日，神舟环宇。告慰先祖，盛世在即。

大同世界，四海兄弟。世界和平，假年可期！

伏惟尚飨，为祷为祈！

2004 年 9 月 28 日，时任曲阜市委副书记、市长江成恭读祭文。　　　（图片由济宁日报社提供）

On September 28th, 2004, Jiang Cheng, Deputy Secretary of the CPC Qufu Municipal Committee and Mayor of Qufu at that time, solemnly recited the commemoration text.

◎ 注释

1. 物阜民熙：物产富饶，人民安乐。形容升平景象。

2. 居安思危：处于安宁的环境中，要想到可能出现的危难。《左传·襄公十一年》："《书》曰：'居安思危。'思则有备，有备无患。"

3. 纲纪：法度；纲常。《汉书·礼乐志》："夫立君臣，等上下，使纲纪有序，六亲和睦，此非天之所为，人之所设也。" 梁启超《论中国之将强》："西人之将灭人国也，则必上之于议院，下之于报章，日日言其国政之败坏，纲纪之紊乱。"

4. 兼济：各方面都擅长。晋·潘岳《杨荆州诔》："草隶兼善，尺牍必珍。"

5. 春晖：春日的阳光，比喻深厚的恩情。

6. 桃李：《韩诗外传》卷七："夫春树桃李，夏得阴其下，秋得食其实。"后遂以"桃李"比喻栽培的后辈和所教的门生。

7. 三坟五典：传说中我国最古的书籍。《左传·昭公十二年》："是能读三坟、五典、八索、九丘。"

8. 六经：六部儒家经典。即《礼》《乐》《诗》《书》《易》《春秋》。《庄子·天运》："孔子谓老聃曰：'丘治《诗》《书》《礼》《乐》《易》《春秋》六经，自以为久矣，孰知其故矣。'"

9. 见贤思齐：看到德才兼备的人，就想向他学习，和他一样。《论语·里仁》："子曰：'见贤思齐焉，见不贤而内自省也。'"

10. 依仁志道，据德游艺：以道为志向，以德为根据，以仁为依靠，以艺为游憩。《论语·述而》："子曰：志于道，据于德，依于仁，游于艺。"

11. 见利思义：看到利益，想到道义。谓以道义为重。《论语·宪问》："见利思义，见危授命，久要不忘平生之言，亦可以为成人矣！"

12. 刚健：坚强有力。《易·乾》："大哉乾乎！刚健中正，纯粹精也。"孔颖达疏："谓纯阳刚健，其性刚强，其行劲健。"

13. 自强不息：自己努力向上，永不停息。《易·乾》："天行健，君子以自强不息。"

14. 通衢：四通八达的道路。汉·班昭《东征赋》："遵通衢之大道兮，求捷径欲从谁。"

15. 近悦远来：近居的人悦服，远处的人慕化而来。形容政治清明，远近归附。《论语·子路》："叶公问政，子曰：'近者说，远者来。'"邢炳疏："子曰：当施惠于近者，使之喜说，则远者当慕化而来也。"

16. 老养壮用：出自《礼记·礼运》："老有所终，壮有所用，幼有所长，矜寡孤独废疾者，皆有所养。"

17. 兆民：古称天子之民，后泛指民众、百姓。《书·吕刑》："一人有庆，兆民赖之。"《礼记·月令》："〔孟春之月〕命相布德和令，行庆施惠，下及兆民。"郑玄注："天子曰兆民。"

◎ 译文

公元2004年9月28日，农历甲申年中秋时节，先师孔子诞辰2555年，曲阜各界代表、海内外宾朋、孔子后裔，肃立在大成殿前，恭敬地用鲜花雅乐庄重地祭祀先师孔子。祭文是：

孔子被称为文化圣人，他所创立的儒家文化影响到海内外。他是千古巨人，万世先师。在繁荣昌盛的时代，物产富饶，人民安乐。然而，高岸耸立，修长的秀竹怕失去节制。我们应该居安思危，振作起来重新制定规则。在以德治国的同时，法治与德治相结合、相促进。

孔子被后人奉为楷模。他的学说贯通古今，道德比肩天地。孔子在杏坛设教，恩泽后代，礼乐文化在泮池传播，弟子众多。这里有"三坟""五典""六经"等古籍。古老文化的传承，薪火相传了千百年。如今我们这一代人，也要学习前贤，和他们一样。

我们肩负着重大的责任，要继承弘扬中华优秀传统文化。以道为志向，以德为根据，以仁为依靠，以艺为游憩。以仁为己任，看到利益时以道义为重。追求中庸的道德境界，避免过犹不及的极端行为。与各国和睦相处，共同发展，摒弃暴戾的行为。刚健有为，自强不息，与时俱进，保持创新的活力。

清风吹遍神州大地，人们精神振奋，像骏马一样驰骋。文化名城曲阜，道路平整，四通八达。绿树茂盛，花团锦簇，绽放芬芳，各个行业繁荣昌盛，日新月异。让近处的人心悦诚服，远处的人自动到来，修身齐家，治国平天下。老人得到赡养，壮者发挥才能，百姓都能生活幸福。孔子故里儒风犹在。

慎重对待身后的事，追思先祖的教诲，为国家的繁荣贡献力量。继承前人的智慧，凝聚共同的志向。东方巨龙腾飞，有人民奋斗的力量。海水深广有鲸鲵吞舟吐浪，凤凰鼓翼而舞，神舟飞船遨游天际。告慰孔子，我们即将迎来盛世。大同世界的理想社会，天下人皆同手足，亲如一家，世界和平将成为现实。伏请您享用供品！

祭孔大典现场　　　　　（图片由济宁日报社提供）

The scene of Confucius Commemoration Ceremony.

Text of the Jiashen Year (2004) Confucius Commemoration Ceremony

Written by: David Yang Zuoren

On the Gregorian Calendar, today is September 28, 2004. On the Chinese Lunar Calendar, it is the middle of autumn in the Year of the Wood Monkey. Our great teacher, Confucius, was born 2,555 years ago. People from all over Qufu, domestic and international guests, friends, and descendants of Confucius, stand solemnly in front of the Dacheng Hall. Accompanied by flowers and elegant music, we respectfully pay tribute to our departed Master.

As it is written:

Ancestral literary Sage, benefactor of the world. A giant throughout the ages and a teacher for all generations.

A prosperous age is a joyous time; there is social stability, and everyone lives and works in peace and contentment. Even though everything looks beautiful from afar, disorder and malcontent may lurk in the shadows.

Even in times of peace and prosperity, we should be ready for danger and practice discipline. The country is governed with virtue, and the name of that virtue is the law.

Thanks must be given to the sages and philosophers who have come before us and whose wisdom has been passed down throughout the generations. Knowledge passes from ancient to modern times, and the virtue of Heaven is brought to Earth.

The warm light of the Apricot Altar shines forth like the sun on a spring day; the Academy Pond is surrounded by the fruit of our teacher's labor. The canonical classics of antiquity lit the spark of a fire that has burned unceasingly for generation upon generation. Now, our generation recognizes wisdom and thinks deeply about it.

Our burden is heavy, and the road is long, but the legacy must be carried forward. We should behave with benevolence and wisdom and adhere to morality with our pleasures.

We must be benevolent. When we realize there will be financial benefits, we must consider the moral cost. Doing too much is the same as not doing enough. Instead, it is necessary to do precisely as must be done.

Seek harmony between all factions and rebuke violent deeds and actions. Vigorous strength, self-knowledge, and constantly striving for self-improvement are the starting point and prerequisite for realizing self-worth.

Move forward in accordance with the times, and innovate with vitality. A cool breeze blows across the whole land; the people are excited and enthusiastic. The streets and avenues of a famous cultural city are paved with stones, the green trees are covered in blossoms, and the air is perfumed with their scent. All industries are prospering, and new developments and changes are occurring daily.

Cultivating the self, managing family and country well, and appeasing the ordinary people's aspirations in the world is good news that will spread far and wide. All should be willing to endure hardship and privation for the benefit of the old and young alike.

In the hometown of the Sage, the wisdom of those who came before us remains eternally bright. In the fight to strengthen our motherland, act cautiously in pursuit of success.

United with the same virtue, carry on the past and open up the future. The great Oriental Dragon is roaring and rising.

The strength of my shoulders bears a burden as significant as the weight of the sky upon the ocean. The tide rages like a whale spitting water, and the red phoenix's wings are flapping. To catch the moon, to chase the sun, to dream of greatness, and to do the impossible.

In comforting us, our ancestors predicted that an age of prosperity and great flourishing was coming.

In the hopes of a world of great harmony, along with my brothers from all over the world, I wish for world peace and a time of jubilee! Of this, I beseech thee, and I now ask everyone to join me in prayer!

杨佐仁简介

　　杨佐仁：1954年生，著名旅美学者、作家、诗人，美国植物医药联盟主席，曾任曲阜师范大学历史系教授，山东儒商学院院长，世界孔子基金会会长。从2004年曲阜首次公祭孔子开始，到2007年，连续四年撰写《祭孔子文》。

　　研究领域：孔子思想和文字学研究。

　　主要著作：长篇历史文学传记《孔子传》，英文著作《The Global Confucius》（世界的孔子），创作孔子电视片《孔子与中国》，联合出版《孔子教育思想论文集》。

Introduction to David Yang Zuoren

David Yang Zuoren, born in 1954 and residing in America, is a Chinese scholar, writer, poet, and Chairman of the American Association of Plant Medicine. He previously served as a professor in the History Department of Qufu Normal University and as the Director of the Shandong Confucian Business Institute. He is also the President of the World Confucius Foundation. From the first public Confucius Memorial Ceremony in Qufu in 2004 until 2007, he was the author of the "Confucius Memorial Ceremony Script" for four consecutive years.

Research Area: Confucian thoughts and philology.

Major Works: His major works include the lengthy historical literary biography "The Life of Confucius," the English book "The Global Confucius," and the creation of the television series "Confucius and China." He also co-published the collection of essays "Confucian Educational Thought."

2005 乙酉年

弘扬优秀传统文化

构建文明和谐社会　促进开放创新发展

2005, the Year of Yiyou.
Promoting excellent traditional culture, building a civilized harmonious
society, and fostering open, innovative development.

纪念孔子诞辰
2556 年

Commemorating the 2556th Anniversary of Confucius's Birth

乙酉（2005）年祭孔大典祭文

杨佐仁　撰

　　维公元二〇〇五年九月二十八日，岁次乙酉，孔子诞辰两千五百五十六年，曲阜市各界人士、海内外宾朋、孔子后裔，满怀崇敬之情，谨备鲜花雅乐，恭祭我中华先师。其文曰：

　　海右[1]山东，岱南奎星[2]。垣墙环抱，岸柳梳拢。
玉树攀云，紫叶吟虹。水含苔浦，草铺莺鸣。
歌动八垠[3]，舞牵九瀛[4]。全球祭孔，五州同风。
设奖开坛，薪火传承。春秋绝笔[5]，诗礼趋庭[6]。

　　植桧葳蕤，宅井鸿蒙。高山景行，杏坛筵盈。
文脉绵延，海域再兴。百所学院，有孔命名。
千年儒流，今古汇通。天人合一[7]，与时偕行。
仁者爱人，和而不同[8]。阴阳和谐，执两用中[9]。

　　和生万物，万物和兴。天道和运，地势和行。
家国和睦，世界和平。圣城曲阜，物阜文丰。

华夏标志，百里新城。政通人和 [10]，德道常青。
小康初成，大同在梦。欣逢盛世，强国威风。

宝岛盼归，华夏一统。旭日中天，巨龙飞腾。
鲲犁碧海，鹏登蟾宫。四海翘首，八方叹惊。
继往开来，待我后生！伏维尚飨！

2005 年 9 月 28 日，时任曲阜市委副书记、市长江成恭读祭文。　　　（图片由济宁日报社提供）

On September 28th, 2005, Jiang Cheng, Deputy Secretary of the CPC Qufu Municipal Committee and Mayor of Qufu at that time, solemnly recited the commemoration text.

◎ 注释

1. 海右：指黄河、东海以西地区。方位以西为右，故称。南朝·梁·江淹《恨赋》："方架鼋鼍以为梁，巡海右以送日。"唐·杜甫《陪李北海宴历下亭》："海右此亭古，济南名士多。"

2. 奎星：按古人的天文学说，二十八宿中的奎星，是专门主管文运之神。从星相图看，奎星屈曲相钩，似文字之画。

3. 八垠：八方的界限。《魏书·高允传》："四海从风，八垠渐化。"唐·杜甫《寄薛三郎中（据）》诗："赋诗宾客间，挥洒动八垠。"

4. 九瀛：（1）指九州与环其外的瀛海。唐·陈子昂《蓟丘览古》诗："邹子何寥廓，漫说九瀛垂。"（2）泛指海外各国。宋·罗泌《路史·后纪十·黄帝》："九瀛仰化，诸北贡职，杨裘柜鬯，贯匈长股，莫不来庭而依朔。"

5. 春秋绝笔：春秋时期鲁哀公十四年猎获麒麟。相传孔子作《春秋》至此而辍笔。《春秋·哀公十四年》："春，西狩获麟。"杜预注："麟者，仁兽，圣王之嘉瑞也。时无明王，出而遇获，仲尼伤周道之不兴，感嘉瑞之无应，故因《鲁春秋》而修中兴之教。绝笔于'获麟'之一句，所感而作，固所以为终也。"

6. 诗礼趋庭：比喻诗礼相传。《论语·季氏》："尝独立，鲤趋而过庭。曰：'学《诗》乎？'对曰'未也。''不学《诗》，无以言。'鲤退而学《诗》。他日，又独立，鲤趋而过庭。曰：'学《礼》乎？'对曰：'未也。''不学《礼》，无以立。'鲤退而学《礼》。"

7. 天人合一：中国哲学中关于天人关系的一种观点。与"天人之分"说相对立。认为"天"有意志，人事是天意的体现；天意能支配人事，人事能感动天意，由此两者合为一体。战国时子思、孟子首先明确提出这种理论，汉儒董仲舒继承此说，发展为"天人感应"论。

8. 和而不同：谓和衷共济，而又各有所见，不苟同于人。《论语·子路》："君子和而不同，小人同而不和。"三国·魏何晏《论语集解》："君子心和，然其所见各异，故曰不同。"

9. 执两用中：儒家思想中的一个重要概念，强调在处理问题时，要把握事物的两个方面，然后采用适中的方法，达到中和状态。《礼记·中庸》："执其两端，用其中于民，其斯以为舜乎？"

10. 政通人和：政事顺遂，人民和乐。宋·范仲淹《岳阳楼记》："政通人和，百废俱兴。"

◎ 译文

公元二〇〇五年九月二十八日，农历乙酉年，孔子诞辰两千五百五十六年，曲阜市各界人士、海内外宾朋、孔子后裔，满怀崇敬之情，恭敬地准备了鲜花雅乐，祭祀中华先师。祭文是：

在东海以西的山东，泰山以南，奎星对应鲁国的区域。城墙环绕，岸边垂柳在风中依依摇动，树木高耸入云，紫叶欢快地吟唱。河水覆盖着绿苔，芳草如茵，莺鸣婉转。

祭孔大典的乐舞响彻八方大地，牵动着海内外，全球各地都在同时祭孔。我们设立了"联合国教科文组织孔子教育奖"奖项，开设了论坛，让孔子的智慧得以传承。孔子著作春秋，教诲诗礼，使文化相传承。

孔庙的桧树苍翠茂盛，宅井仍在。我们尊崇孔子，共同站立在杏坛前。文脉绵延不绝，在海内外再次兴起。百所学院兴起，都以孔子的名字来命名。

千年的儒学流脉，汇通着古今。人与天相应，与时代同行。仁者爱人，君子相和而不相同。阴阳二气和谐，把握对立面而取其中道。和能生万物，万物因和而繁荣。天的规律因和谐而运转，地的规律因和谐而运行。家国和睦，世界和平。圣城曲阜物产丰富，文化繁荣。远近百里的地方，正在建设成为华夏文化传承示范新城。政务通达顺利，人民安居乐业，道德如树木常青。

　　小康社会初步建成，大同社会是我们的梦想。我们欣逢盛世，国家强大，威武雄壮。宝岛台湾在盼望回归，华夏一统是众望所归。旭日中天，巨龙翱翔于天际。鲲鱼跃过碧海，鹏鸟登上蟾宫。五湖四海的人们都翘首以盼，八方的人们都为之惊叹。继承过去的精华，迎接未来的挑战，未来待我们书写！伏请您享用供品！

祭孔大典现场　　　　　　（图片由济宁日报社提供）

The scene of Confucius Commemoration Ceremony.

Text of the Yiyou Year (2005) Confucius Commemoration Ceremony

Written by: David Yang Zuoren

On the Gregorian Calendar, today is September 28, 2005. On the Chinese Lunar Calendar, it is the Year of the Wood Rooster. Two thousand, five hundred and fifty-six years have passed since the birth of Confucius. People from Qufu, domestic and international guests, friends, and descendants of Confucius are respectfully accompanied by flowers and elegant music as we pay tribute to our departed Master.

As it is written:

Shandong is bordered by the sea with a holy mountain that scrapes the sky. Shandong is surrounded by willow-lined coasts.

Shandong, where the Silver Jade Plant climbs to the clouds, and the Cherry Plum reaches for the rainbow. Shandong, where mossy waters are home to singing birds whose birdsong moves the heart to a rhythmic beat heard by all the world outside of China.

The Confucian Sacrificial Rites are celebrated worldwide, with every nation celebrating the same founder of ritual who kindled a fire that has already burned unceasingly for generations. Apart from Spring and Autumn Annals, poetry and etiquette have been inherited from the ones who came before us.

Verdant green cypress trees run riot in a courtyard that has existed since ancient times. In the foothills of the tall mountain, the Apricot

Altar is loaded with offerings.

The threads of culture unspool onward and onward, and the land is revitalized. A hundred schools of thought and philosophy are named for Confucius.

A thousand years of Confucianism connect the past and the present. Moving with the times, the heavens and humanity proceed in step.

A benevolent person loves others and harmoniously accepts their differences. Dark and light, yin and yang, all are harmoniously in balance.

When balance is found, harmony is brought to all things. Even when the terrain is rough, the way of Heaven is the way forward.

Peace for the people, for the country, and for all the world's countries. The holy city of Qufu is rich in culture.

A symbol of China and a symbol of the new era. Enlightened politics and proper morals lead to a stable country with happy people.

A well-off society has just begun, and the possibility of Great Harmony is no longer a fleeting dream. Rejoice in a powerful and majestic country for a prosperous age is a joyous time.

China will be reunified, and the precious island will be welcomed home. The rising sun is in the sky. The hard years have passed, and the good days have just arrived. The great dragon is not only awake but soaring.

Ascending to the imperial examination hall, the tests have been written and passed. Across the world, and to everyone's amazement, the wings of hope have taken flight.

Carry on from the past, open up for the future, and wait for my descendants! I give thanks again and again!

2006 丙戌年

弘扬优秀传统文化

加强两岸文化交流　促进开放合作发展

2006, the Year of Bingxu.
Promoting excellent traditional culture, enhancing cross-strait cultural communications, and fostering open, cooperative development.

纪念孔子诞辰
2557
年

Commemorating the 2557th Anniversary of Confucius's Birth

丙戌（2006）年祭孔大典祭文

杨佐仁　撰

岁在丙戌，节届仲秋。先师诞辰，二五五七。曲阜人民，孔子后裔，两岸同胞，四海宾朋，大成殿前，肃穆祭孔。文曰：

洙泗流带，沃野万垄。尼峄滴翠，回峰千重。
白云舒卧，紫霞纵横。红缠杏坛，绿掩碑亭。
古城墉堞[1]，圣庙龙腾。诞圣吉日，鼓乐奏鸣。
嘉卉六醴，果饼三牲。童子俎豆[2]，耄耋礼容。
同根一脉，两岸祭孔。共缅先师，追远慎终。
志道据德[3]，心正意诚。节用爱民[4]，修齐治平。
为政北辰[5]，身正令行[6]。见利思义，后凋寒松。
近悦远来，躬身自省。博文约礼[7]，弘毅任重。
己所不欲，勿施人行。仁义宅居，诚信轫[8]衡。
忠孝首善，礼法持恒。中道不倚，恕道宽容。
以和为贵，华夏一统。乾坤氤氲，和谐化生。
天和雨行，地和物丰。家和事兴，国和人定。
万邦和谐，世界和平。遗训在耳，发聩振聋。

高山仰止[9]，桴海道兴。联合国奖，以孔命名。

亘古首屈，文教巅峰。百所学院，遍及九瀛。

黄发碧目，学在泮宫[10]。五洲四海，章甫[11]诵经。

赞誉远播，天下服膺。故里乡亲，蹈德践行。

幼学长教，老养壮用。诚信工商，让畔桑农。

居如图藻，行掣电风。盛世再现，小康初成。

天枹击鼓，海钹震庭。河山舞姿，日月霓虹。

龙飙鳞爪，凤翥翼翀。魂兮归来，又梦大同。

伏惟尚飨！

　　2006 年 9 月 28 日，时任曲阜市委副书记、市长
江成恭读祭文。　　　　　　（图片由济宁日报社提供）

On September 28th, 2006, Jiang Cheng, Deputy Secretary of the CPC Qufu Municipal Committee and Mayor of Qufu at that time, solemnly recited the commemoration text.

◎ 注释

1. 堞堞：女墙，城墙上的矮墙。亦泛指城墙。

2. 俎豆：（1）俎和豆，古代祭祀、宴会时盛食物的两种器皿，亦泛指各种礼器。（2）引申为祭祀和崇奉之意。《论语·卫灵公》：卫灵公问陈于孔子。孔子对曰："俎豆之事，则尝闻之矣；军旅之事，未之学也。"

3. 志道据德：以道为志向，以德为根据，以仁为依靠，以艺为游憩。《论语·述而》："子曰：'志于道，据于德，依于仁，游于艺。'"

4. 节用爱民：节省开支，爱护百姓。出自《论语·学而》，子曰："道千乘之国，敬事而信，节用而爱人，使民以时。"

5. 北辰：北极星。《论语·为政》，子曰："为政以德，譬如北辰，居其所而众星共之。"

6. 身正令行：《论语·子路》："子曰：其身正，不令而行；其身不正，虽令不从。"

7. 博文约礼：广求学问，恪守礼法。《论语·雍也》："君子博学于文，约之以礼，亦可以弗畔矣夫！"

8. 轫：支住车轮不使旋转的木头。

9. 高山仰止：高山，比喻高尚的品德。也比喻对高尚的品德的仰慕。《诗·小雅·车辖》："高山仰止，景行行止。"

10. 泮宫：古代的国家高等学校。

11. 章甫：古代一种礼帽。

◎ 译文

丙戌年仲秋时节，适逢先师孔子诞辰 2557 年，曲阜人民、孔子后裔、两岸同胞、四海宾朋齐聚大成殿前，庄严肃穆地祭祀孔子。祭文是：

洙泗河流经之地，有着肥沃的土地和万亩良田。尼山和峄山的翠绿山峰，仿佛是千层环绕的山峰。白云舒展着，像在躺着休息，紫色的云霞纵横交错。铺满红色鲜花的杏坛和被绿植掩映的碑亭相互映衬。古城的城墙，孔庙的龙腾尽显庄重。

在这神圣、吉祥的日子里，击鼓声和奏乐声一齐响起。鲜花、六种美酒、水果、点心和用于祭祀的牛、羊、猪全都供奉在祭坛上。小孩子们手持祭祀用的礼器，长者们遵循礼制，以庄重的仪容出席。两岸人民同属一脉，共同祭祀孔子，一起缅怀这位伟大的先师，追忆他的深远影响并虔诚地祭奠他。

以道为志向，以德为根据，心怀正义、态度真诚，节省开支、爱护百姓，真正通过提升自身修养、整治好家庭、治理好国家后实现社会和谐、太平。凭着自身的道德修养管理国家，就会像北极星被众星环绕那样，只有自身端正，才能让百姓信服并跟随。面对利益时要想到道义的要求，要像寒冬的松树一样坚忍不拔。让周围的人感到愉悦，就会吸引远方的人前来，同时应该谦虚谨慎，不断反省自己的言行，改进提升。广泛学习各种知识、遵守礼法规范，要有远大的志向、坚强的意志，勇于担当责任的精神品质。学会换位思考和尊重他人，自己不愿意承受的事情，不可以强加给别人。

以仁义为根本、诚信为支撑，注重忠诚和孝顺，遵守礼法和道德规范，保持中庸之道的同时，也要宽容大度，以和为贵，只有和谐统一才能真正实现国家繁荣。宇宙万物都在和谐中生长、发展，只有天地万物都处于和谐状态，才能得到充分的滋养。家庭和睦，所有事情都会兴旺发达，国家和谐，百姓的心才能安定，国与国之间和谐，世界才能和平安定，我们要时刻铭记这些遗留下来的宝贵教诲，让它们引导我们的言行举止。崇高的道德值得我们仰慕，而对智慧和真理的追求，要像坐筏子渡海一样。

联合国教科文组织"孔子教育奖"是有史以来第一次以孔

祭孔大典现场　　　　　　　（图片由济宁日报社提供）

The scene of Confucius Commemoration Ceremony.

子命名的奖项，是文化和教育的巅峰。近百所孔子学院，遍布全球各地，来自五湖四海的老人、小孩都在这里接受传统文化的熏陶，共同诵读经典。孔子学院在国内外赢得了广泛的赞誉和认可。

　　曲阜人民也注重道德品质、知识技能的培养。小孩子受到良好教育，年轻人得到成长机会为社会做贡献，老年人得到赡养。工商业活动中尽显诚信，农业方面也有良好的发展，居住环境优美如画，出行速度也快如闪电，繁荣昌盛的时代重现，小康社会初步形成。鼓声震天，海浪激荡，大山大河摇曳生姿，在日月的照耀下也出现彩虹。龙凤翱翔，是大展宏图的姿态，回归本真，一同追寻那个和谐、美好的社会。

　　伏请您享用供品！

Text of the Bingxu Year (2006) Confucius Commemoration Ceremony

Written by: David Yang Zuoren

On the Chinese Lunar Calendar, it is the middle of autumn in the Year of the Fire Dog. It is also the 2557th birthday of our departed Master. People in Qufu, descendants of Confucius, compatriots on both sides of the Taiwan Straits, and friends from all over the world solemnly stand together in front of the Dacheng Hall to pay our respects to Confucius.

As it is written:

Home to the Confucian Schools, the Zhu-Si River Valley is a fertile and green place. Beneath a sky dotted with white clouds and rose mist in the light of the rising sun, a thousand folded mountain peaks are furred with jade growth.

Vermilion is the Apricot Altar. Emerald is the Stele Pavilion.

On the ancient walls of the city, the roaring sound of the celebration is heard from the Confucius Temple. It is the Master's birthday. The drums sound like the wings of birds beating in unison.

Offerings of fruit, chicken, fish, and pork are being made. The gifts of youth become the wisdom of old age.

Born of the same roots, both sides of the Straits participate in the Confucian Sacrificial Rites. Cautiously pursuing our mutual goals, we devoutly commemorate our departed Master.

Aspire to the truth of the Tao, and base your actions on virtue, choose benevolence, be upright and sincere in thought and deed. Spend prudently and care for the people, cultivate the self, manage your family and country well, and appease the common people's aspirations.

Govern the empire with virtue and act accordingly. When we realize there is a financial benefit, we must consider the moral cost. Otherwise, disaster may befall us.

Good news spreads both far and wide; genuflect to the masters and reflect on yourself. Seeking knowledge widely and abiding by proper etiquette, strength of mind, and character are heavy burdens.

Follow the Golden Rule. Don't do to others what you don't want them to do to you. Benevolence and righteousness are built upon a foundation of integrity.

Loyalty and filial piety are the primary virtues, and etiquette and law are eternal. Be tolerant of others, but don't stray too far towards appeasement.

Peace and unification is the most important thing. Everything, including the seeds of harmony, can be found between Heaven and Earth.

The seasons of sun and the seasons of rain have come in their proper time, and the Earth has fruitful abundance. When harmony is found at the household level, all is prosperous. When the country is harmonious, the people experience great benefits.

World peace will come when all factions find common ground. With the Master's words of wisdom in our ears, our consciousness is awoken.

With character, talent, and knowledge as tall as a mountain, be the kind of person others look up to and inspire others to flourish. Across the globe, hundreds of institutes of higher education have been established in Confucius's name. He has been representative of the pinnacle of culture and education ever since antiquity; even UNESCO has a prize named after him.

All lands touched by the seven seas are home to flaxen-haired scholars diligently learning and repeating his words.

Words of praise are cast far and wide, and the whole world knows his name. As sons of the same soil, from suckling babe to old age, we wholeheartedly practice and study virtue all the days of our lives. The grace of kings is not limited to kings. All must practice integrity in industry and commerce.

People's living standards and environment have improved significantly, and travel methods have become more efficient and convenient. A prosperous period in history has once again begun, and the early stages of a well-off society are slowing in all respects.

Heaven's drumsticks beat a rat-a-tat pattern as Earth's cymbals shake the ground. The rivers and mountains dance, and the sun and moon put on a light show.

The dragon soars. The phoenix flies. Trivial and insignificant things fall by the wayside. Happiness and prosperity are achieved. Our spirits have found their calling, and the dream of Great Harmony is beckoning.

I respectfully beseech you!

2007 丁亥年

走近孔子　喜迎奥运
同根一脉　共建和谐

2007, the Year of Dinghai.
Embracing the Olympics with Confucius,
building harmony together with the same root.

纪念孔子诞辰2558年

Commemorating the 2558th Anniversary of Confucius's Birth

丁亥（2007）年祭孔大典祭文

杨佐仁　撰

　　清风送爽，海晏河清。国泰民安，举国欢腾。时逢中华文化先祖孔子诞辰 2558 周年，海内外宾朋，世界各地华人华侨，港澳台同胞，谨备鲜花礼乐，肃立于曲阜孔庙大成殿前，恭祭孔子诞辰。其文曰：

海右 [1] 山东，岱南奎星。圣诞吉日，鼓乐奏鸣。
黄河讴歌，泰山挺松。飞泉漱液，嘉卉吐红。
日月增光，齐鲁夸荣。西振河源，东澹海瀛。
北动玄土，南耀朱岭。环球华裔，额首隆庆。
侨胞同胞，根连脉通。亚非欧美，百校名孔。
奥林匹克，喜临京城。五洲四海，睹我雄风。
大同非梦，人类有情。圣哲先导，万邦 [2] 风从。
我辈协力，盛世太平。风发飙扬，纛 [3] 拂云中。
天地人和，万物繁盛。与时偕进，和谐化生。
天和雨顺，地和物丰。家和事兴，国和人定。
仁者爱人 [4]，和而不同 [5]。忠孝首善，修齐治平。
为政以德，气正风清。见利思义，躬行自省。

政通人和[6]，德道常青。农工商旅，百业同兴。

教科文卫，人本民生。生态环保，天人一行。

原隰[7]郁茂，畎渎[8]流清。芳草绿堤，粳谷盈丰。

城如蜃楼，货殖纵横。翰墨奋藻，学子书英。

大国崛起，自强不陵。一飞冲天，华夏振兴。

励精图治[9]，众志成城。万代功业，待我后生！

伏惟尚飨！

2007 年 9 月 28 日，时任山东省委副书记、代省长姜大明恭读祭文。 （图片由济宁日报社提供）

On September 28th, 2007, Jiang Daming, Deputy Secretary of the CPC Shandong Provincial Committee and Acting Governor of Shandong Province at that time, solemnly recited the commemoration text.

◎ 注释

1. 海右：山东在古代的雅称。指黄河、东海以西地区。

2. 万邦：所有诸侯封国，后引申为天下、全国。

3. 纛：（1）古代用羽毛做的舞具或帝王车舆上的饰物。（2）古时军队或仪仗队的大旗。

4. 仁者爱人：《孟子·离娄下》第二十八章："仁者爱人，有礼者敬人。"

5. 和而不同：和，和睦；同，苟同。指和睦地相处，但不随便附和。《论语·子路》："君子和而不同，小人同而不和。"

6. 政通人和：政治开明，百姓和睦；形容国家稳定，人民安乐。宋·范仲淹《岳阳楼记》："越明年，政通人和，百废俱兴。"

7. 原隰：广大平坦和低洼潮湿的地方。

8. 畎渎：田间沟渠。《后汉书·文苑传上·杜笃》："畎渎润淤，水泉灌溉，渐泽成川，粳稻陶遂。"

9. 励精图治：励，振奋；图，谋求。努力振奋精神，千方百计治理好国家或干好事业。东汉·班固《汉书·魏相传》："宣帝始亲万机，厉精为治。"

◎ 译文

在这个清风送爽、海晏河清的时刻，国家太平、人民安乐，全国上下共同纪念中华文化先祖孔子诞辰 2558 周年。海内外的宾客朋友、世界各地的华人华侨以及港澳台同胞备好鲜花，庄严肃穆地来到曲阜孔庙大成殿前，恭敬地祭祀孔子诞辰。祭文是：

在东海以西的山东，泰山以南，奎星对应鲁国的区域。在这祭祀孔子神圣、吉祥的日子，击鼓声和奏乐声一齐响起。黄河被我们赞美歌唱，泰山上的青松矗立挺拔，泉水激荡，花草繁茂，绽放色彩。日月星辰更加明亮，齐鲁大地有美丽的容貌。西边振兴黄河源头，东边治理海域，北边保护黑土地，南边有熠熠生辉的南岭。全球的华裔们，心怀谦卑，共同庆祝，海内外侨胞们同属一脉，血脉相通。

近百所孔子学院遍布亚非欧美。奥林匹克运动会即将在北京举行，来自五湖四海的人们会见证我们的实力和风采。只要我们有情有义，实现大同社会就不是梦想。圣哲先贤的教诲全国都在遵从、响应，我们要齐心协力，共同创造兴盛安定的社会，像是狂风中的旗帜，高高地飘扬在云端。

天时地利人和，世界万物才会繁荣和生机。与时俱进，永不停滞，实现和谐共生。天地和谐，才能风调雨顺、资源丰盛。家庭和睦，所有事情就会兴旺发达；国家和谐，百姓的心才能安定。仁慈的人懂得关爱他人，与别人交往时，尊重他人的不同意见和观点，保持和谐的关系。忠诚和孝顺是重要的美德，提升自身修养，整治家庭，治理好国家实现社会和谐太平。以道德治理国家，社会风气才会端正、纯净。面对利益时要想到道义的要求，同时要时常反省自己的言行，改进提升。政治开明、人民和谐，才能保持道德的生命力。

是农业、工业、商业、旅游业，所有的行业共同发展，教育、科技、文化和医疗卫生关系到每个人的日常生活。我们要注重生态环境保护，实现人与自然的和谐共生。广袤的平原上草木郁郁葱葱，田间的沟渠里流淌着清澈的小溪。芳草绿堤，粳稻谷物硕果累累。城市繁华得像蜃楼，商业繁荣发展，文人

祭孔大典现场 　　　　　（图片由济宁日报社提供）

The scene of Confucius Commemoration Ceremony.

墨客挥毫泼墨，青年学子奋发向上。

国家正在崛起，朝着自己努力的方向不松懈。我们要一飞冲天，实现华夏民族的伟大复兴。振奋精神、齐心协力地为国家发展而努力奋斗。创造伟大的事业，需要我们这一代年轻人去完成！

伏请您享用供品！

Text of the Dinghai Year (2007) Confucius Commemoration Ceremony

Written by: David Yang Zuoren

Cool breezes bring succor; the waters of the land are calm and untroubled. The country is peaceful, the people are safe, and everyone is rejoicing. Today is the 2,559th birthday of our ancestral Sage Confucius. Domestic and international guests and friends; people from China and the sons and daughters of Chinese descent from all over the world; compatriots from Hong Kong, Macao and Taiwan; I ask of you to prepare fresh flowers and celebratory music; I ask of you to stand in the courtyard in front of the Dacheng Hall of the Qufu Confucius Temple, I ask of you to respectfully pay tribute to Confucius on this special day.

As it is written:

In a land bordered by the sea with mountains that scrape the sky, it is the Master's birthday. On this day, the ranks of beating drums sound like a flock of birds beating their wings in unison.

Even the Yellow River celebrates. Even Mt. Taishan is happy. As autumn's touch paints the countryside red, water gushes from burbling springs.

Are the sun and moon brighter than before? Is Shandong's glory praised even louder? From the River's source in the west to the sea in the east, a great cry of celebration has gone up!

From the loamy black soil of the north to the cinnabar mountains of the south, a great cry of celebration has gone up! Throughout the world, all descendants of Chinese blood bow their heads in celebration.

By blood, sweat, tears, and mutual history, our countrymen, our compatriots, and all children of Chinese descent are connected. In Asia, Africa, Europe, and America, a hundred institutions of higher education have been opened in Confucius's name.

The Olympic Games will be coming to Beijing. All lands touched by the seven seas will see our glory.

Mankind's achievement of the Great Harmony is no fleeting and impossible dream. All parties acting in compliance with the guidance of the great Sage and working together will undoubtedly lead to prosperous and peaceful times.

The winds of change are blowing, and the banners of joint action are clearing the sky.

All things on Heaven and Earth and all people are prospering. Move forward in accordance with the times and achieve harmony.

The seasons of sun and the seasons of rain have come in their proper time, and the Earth has fruitful abundance. When harmony is found at the household level, all is prosperous. When the country is harmonious, the people experience great benefits.

A benevolent person loves others and harmoniously accepts their differences. Loyalty and filial piety are the primary virtues.Cultivate the self, manage your family and country well, and appease the common people's aspirations.

Govern with virtue and morality and maintain a clean and upright spirit. When we realize there is financial benefit, we must practice introspection and consider the moral cost.

Enlightened politics and proper morals lead to a stable country with happy people. Agriculture, industry, commerce, and tourism sectors are thriving, and education, science, culture, and health are increasingly people-oriented.

Showing that man can live in harmony with nature, awareness of protecting the environment is rising.

The wilderness grows lush, and babbling brooks run clean and clear. Green plants carpet the hillsides, and the valleys are ripe with grain.

Filled with goods, the bustling city is like a beautiful mirage. Students' essays, calligraphy and paintings are both enthusiastic and skilled.

The country is growing stronger and more confident. Soaring towards the sky, the force of China's revitalization is like a rocket lifting off for space.

Hard work and indomitable unity of will are the merits of all generations, including those who have yet to be born!

I respectfully beseech you!

2008 戊子年
仁者爱人　自强不息

2008, the Year of Wuzi.
The Benevolent love others and tirelessly strive for self-improvement.

纪念孔子诞辰 2559 年

Commemorating the 2559th Anniversary of Confucius's Birth

戊子（2008）年祭孔大典祭文

金 庸 撰

岁在戊子，节届国庆，时逢中华文化先祖孔子诞辰2559年，海内外宾朋，港澳台同胞，世界各地华人华侨，谨备鲜花礼乐，肃立于济宁市曲阜孔庙大成殿前，恭祭夫子诞辰，文曰：

清风送爽，海晏河清。国泰民安，举世欢腾。
北京奥运，万邦风从。五洲四海，睹我雄风。
世界同运，人类一梦。中华崛起，国和人定。
为政以德，气正风清。有教无类[1]，修齐治平。
国之将兴，听命于民。博我以文[2]，删正六经[3]。
述而不作，信而好古[4]，为之不厌，不倦诲人[5]。
今我立国，秉承遗教：忠孝首善，礼法持恒，
中道不倚，和恕宽容，以和为贵，华夏一统，
万邦和谐，世界和平。盛世再现，小康初成。
见利思义，仁为己任[6]，中和至德，自强不息。
生态环保，天人一行。夫子圣教，百代维新。
孜孜不懈，永秉传承。伏惟尚飨！

2008 年 9 月 28 日，时任山东省委副书记、省长姜大明恭读祭文。　　　　（图片由济宁日报社提供）

On September 28th, 2007, Jiang Daming, Deputy Secretary of the CPC Shandong Provincial Committee and Governor of Shandong Province at that time, solemnly recited the commemoration text.

◎ 注释

1. 有教无类：指教育不分高低贵贱，对各类人都一视同仁。《论语·卫灵公》："子曰：'有教无类。'"

2. 博我以文：用各种文献来丰富我的知识。《论语·子罕》："夫子循循然善诱人，博我以文，约我以礼，欲罢不能。"

3. 六经：指经过孔子整理而传授的六部先秦古籍，分别为《诗》《书》《礼》《乐》《易》《春秋》。

4. 述而不作，信而好古：述，传述。只阐述而不创作，相信而且喜好古代的东西。出自《论语·述而》，子曰："述而不作，信而好古，窃比于我老彭。"

5. 为之不厌，不倦诲人：《论语·述而》："子曰：'若圣与仁，则吾岂敢？抑为之不厌，诲人不倦，则可谓云尔已矣。'公西华曰：'正唯弟子不能学也。'"

6. 仁为己任：把实现仁德当作是自己的任务。《论语·泰伯》："曾子曰：'士不可以不弘毅，任重而道远。仁以为己任，不亦重乎？死而后已，不亦远乎？'"

◎ 译文

戊子年国庆前夕，适逢中华文化先祖孔子诞辰 2559 年，来自海内外的嘉宾朋友、港澳台同胞以及世界各地的华人华侨都备好鲜花，庄严肃穆地来到济宁曲阜孔庙大成殿前，恭敬地祭祀孔子诞辰。祭文是：

在这个清风送爽、海晏河清的时刻，国家太平、人民安乐，全国上下一片祥和。各国都在积极响应北京奥运会，来自五湖四海的人们见证了我们的实力和风采。奥运会是世界共同的事业，有人类追求的同一个梦想。中华民族正在崛起，国家和平、人民安定。

用道德治理国家，社会风气才清明、端正。教育不分高低贵贱，提升自身修养，整治家庭，治理国家，实现社会和谐太平。在国家将要兴盛的时候，要倾听百姓的心声。用各类文献来丰富我们的知识，包括修改整理过的"六经"。对待传统文化是传承而不是创作，信仰并喜爱古代的文化，传授知识也不会感到厌烦，总是不知疲倦地教导别人。

如今我们治理国家，要遵循先人的教导：注重忠义和孝顺，遵守礼法和道德规范，保持中庸之道的同时，也要和睦宽容，以和为贵，维护华夏民族的团结统一，使国家各民族和谐共处，世界和平稳定。繁荣昌盛的时代重现，小康社会初步形成。面对利益时要想到道义的要求，将仁德作为自己的责任，追求中庸和谐的最高道德标准，努力上进，不松懈。注重生态环境保护，实现人与自然的和谐共生。孔夫子的神圣教诲，历经几千年仍然可以保持革新。我们要勤奋刻苦、毫不懈怠，永远秉持传承先贤的智慧。伏请您享用供品！

祭孔大典现场　　　　　　　　　　（图片由济宁日报社提供）

The scene of Confucius Commemoration Ceremony.

Text of the Wuzi Year (2008) Confucius Commemoration Ceremony

Written by: Louis Cha Leung-yung (Jin Yong)

On the Chinese Lunar Calendar, it is the middle of autumn in the Year of the Earth Rat. Today is both the celebration of our nation's founding and the 2,559th birthday of our ancestral Sage, Confucius. Domestic and international guests and friends; compatriots from Hong Kong, Macao and Taiwan; the sons and daughters of Chinese descent from all over the world, I ask of you to prepare fresh flowers and celebratory music; I ask those of you who are here with me in Jinan to stand in the courtyard in front of the Dacheng Hall of the Qufu Confucius Temple, and respectfully pay tribute to Confucius on this special day.

As it is written:

Cool breezes bring succor; the waters of the land are calm and untroubled. The country is peaceful, the people are safe, and the whole world is rejoicing.

For the Beijing Olympic Games, all parties and factions act with one heart and mind. All lands touched by the seven seas will see our glory.

One hope, one dream, these are the world's destiny and mankind's goals. A rising China brings great benefit to all people.

Cultivate the self, manage your household well, appease the common people's aspirations, govern with virtue and morality, and maintain a clean and upright spirit, and there will be no limit to the things you can learn.

Prosperity for a nation comes from listening to the common man. Compiling the Six Classics, he taught me the beauty of words.

Always happy to teach, narrate, and explain doctrine rather than to create new philosophies, by expounding upon the thoughts of ancient sages, he organized the cultural classics without unnecessary additions or removals.

Modern China has upheld the legacy of the Master's lessons: that loyalty and filial piety are the primary virtues, etiquette and law are eternal, that one must tolerate others without appeasement, and that peace and unification are the most important things.

World peace will come when all factions find common ground. A prosperous period in history has once again begun, and the early stages of a well-off society are slowing in all respects.

We must be benevolent; taking responsibility shows strength of mind and character. When realizing financial benefit exists, we must consider the moral cost. It is necessary to do exactly as must be done, to constantly strive for self-improvement.

Showing that man can live in harmony with nature, awareness of protecting the environment is rising. The great teachings of Confucius are the restoration and revitalization of a hundred generations.

Work tirelessly and uphold the legacy forever. I respectfully beseech you!

金庸简介

金　庸：1924 年生，原名查良镛，浙江海宁人，1948 年移居香港，当代知名武侠小说作家、新闻学家、企业家、政治评论家、社会活动家，中国作家协会名誉副主席，原浙江大学人文学院院长，香港《明报》创办人，《中华人民共和国香港特别行政区基本法》主要起草人之一，香港最高荣誉"大紫荆勋章"获得者，荣获影响世界华人终身成就奖。

2018 年 10 月 30 日，金庸在香港逝世，享年 94 岁。

主要著作：出版《飞狐外传》《雪山飞狐》《连城诀》《天龙八部》《射雕英雄传》《白马啸西风》《鹿鼎记》《笑傲江湖》《书剑恩仇录》《神雕侠侣》《侠客行》《倚天屠龙记》《碧血剑》《鸳鸯刀》（"飞雪连天射白鹿，笑书神侠倚碧鸳"）及《越女剑》等 15 部武侠小说；出版《金庸散文集》；主编《明报月刊》"明月四十年精品文丛"，囊括《中国戏剧大师的命运》《四海红楼（上下卷）》《大家》《异乡人的星空》等，是《明报月刊》40 年来经典文章的总集。

Introduction to Louis Cha Leung-yung (Jin Yong)

Louis Cha Leung-yung, who is known by his pen name Jin Yong, born in 1924 as Cha Liangyong in Haining, Zhejiang Province, relocated to Hong Kong in 1948. He is a well-known modern martial arts novelist, journalist, entrepreneur, political commentator, and social activist. Jin Yong served as the Honorary Vice Chairman of the China Writers Association, former Director of the Humanities Academy at Zhejiang University, founder of the Hong Kong newspaper "Ming Pao," and one of the main drafters of the "The Basic Law of the Hong Kong Special Administrative Region of the People's Republic of China." He was awarded the highest honor in Hong Kong, the Grand Bauhinia Medal, and received the Lifetime Achievement Award for influencing the global Chinese community. On October 30, 2018, Jin Yong passed away in Hong Kong at the age of 94. His major works include 15 martial arts novels such as "Flying Fox of Snowy Mountain," "A Deadly Secret," "Demi-Gods and Semi-Devils," "The Smiling, Proud Wanderer," "The Legend of the Condor Heroes," and "The Heaven Sword and Dragon Saber." He also published a collection of essays titled "Essays by Jin Yong." Additionally, he edited the "Ming Pao Monthly Magazine 40th Anniversary Collection," which includes classics such as "The Fate of Chinese Drama Masters," "Four Seas Red Mansions" (Volumes I and II), "Everyone," and "The Starry Sky of Strangers," serving as a comprehensive collection of classic articles from the past 40 years of "Ming Pao Monthly Magazine."

2009 己丑年
和衷共济　讲信修睦

2009, the Year of Jichou.
Pull together for a common cause, have faith and promote good will.

纪念孔子诞辰

2560

年

Commemorating the 2560th Anniversary of Confucius's Birth

己丑（2009）年祭孔大典祭文

范 曾 撰

周室颓隳，礼乐废弛，九州失驭。战伐出于诸侯，列国窥窃神器[1]。

春秋之末，仲尼起于陬邑，感万方之多难，乃驰驱以宣教。冀辅弼于乱世，欲敦厉[2]于黎庶。然则宫寝邃远，王者不悟。有楚狂接舆[3]歌而过之，痛詈凤德之衰，切悲庙堂之殆。往者不谏，来者可追，孔子乃归鲁，不复出游。

述而不作，非谓徒托空言[4]，追往事，思来者，悬明镜而作《春秋》[5]，立极[6]则以昭万代。凤鸟不至，河图不出[7]，忧古道之不彰也；久矣吾不复梦见周公，伤往哲之益远也。遂力倡仁恕中和之道，克己复礼[8]之德。

播雨杏坛，天下士赴之如万类之附麟凤。若颜渊、子路、公冶长、有子、子张、子贡、曾子七十二贤列坐其次，三千学子，相望于道。仲尼自云："吾少也贱，故多能鄙事。"乃谆谆以告诸君子，知任重而道远，期弘毅以自励。世幽昧[9]以炫耀，独好古而敏求[10]。视富贵如浮云，思贤若渴，闻义即徙[11]。不降其志，不辱其身。夫子者，其集微子、箕子、比干之懿德嘉行于一身者也。世人以夫子为木铎，非无由也。颜渊喟然而叹曰："仰之弥高，钻之弥坚。瞻之在前，忽焉在后。"是高弟子之敬仰，亦足为万代所共祀者也。荆玉含宝，幽兰怀馨，此孔学之无尽藏也。

延越百余载，孟子起于邹而倡义，与孔子之倡仁相辅佐。又越三百载，汉武独崇儒术，乃有毛亨、郑玄之辈为之诠，董仲舒之属演其说。再越千二百年，南宋理宗[12]朝濂、洛、关、闽[13]之学，勉心景迹，遂成大观，共祭诸孔庙。更越千载，日月虽迈，诵说犹馨，百川竞乎孔子之门庭，孔学之克守，于今愈胜。孔子学院，遍列全球，蔚为人类文化之奇观。

世变事异，而孔学不衰者，以"仁者爱人""先欲达人"为黾勉天下之襟抱；"己所不欲，勿施于人"则厚望瀛海以高节。唯和衷以共济，讲信而修睦。此足称万国邦交之极则，亦各族和谐之宏观。遗训虽远，践行在迩，岁寒松柏，历千万龄而不凋，其非孔子博怀之远猷，而周瞻之大略欤？

巍巍[14]陵寝，郁郁巨柏，云霄万古，黛色参天。仰瞻烟霞，伏增肃敬，焚香再拜，赋以永祷。

◎ **注释**

1. 神器：地位、政权。
2. 敦厉：亦作"敦励"，劝勉、勉励。

2009 年 9 月 28 日，时任山东省委副书记、省长姜大明恭读祭文。 （图片由济宁日报社刘项清拍摄）

On September 28th, 2009, Jiang Daming, Deputy Secretary of the CPC Shandong Provincial Committee and Governor of Shandong Province at that time, solemnly recited the commemoration text.

3. 楚狂接舆：陆通，字接舆，春秋时楚国著名隐士。《论语·微子》："楚狂接舆歌而过孔子曰：'凤兮凤兮！何德之衰？往者不可谏，来者犹可追。已而，已而！今之从政者殆而！'"

4. 徒托空言：指只讲空话，而不实行。《史记·太史公自序》："子曰：'我欲载之空言，不如见之于行事之深切著明也。'"

5.《春秋》：由孔子编订的鲁国史，中国最早的编年体史书。全书大约 17000 字，内容记载春秋时期统治阶级的政治活动、自然现象、经济文化等。

6. 立极：（1）树立最高准则。（2）登帝位；秉国政。

7. 凤鸟不至，河图不出：河图，传说圣人受命，黄河就出现图画，即八卦图。《论语·子罕》："子曰：'凤鸟不至，河不出图，吾已矣夫！'"

8. 克己复礼：克制自己，使自己的言论、行为都符合礼制。《论语·颜渊》："颜渊问仁。子曰：'克己复礼为仁。一日克己复礼，天下归仁焉！为仁由己，而由人乎哉？'"

9. 幽昧：指昏暗不明。

10. 好古而敏求：《论语·述而》："我非生而知之者，好古，敏以求之者也。"

11. 闻义即徙：听到符合道义的事就心动神往，虚心相就。《论语·述而》："德之不修，学之不讲，闻义不能徙，不善不能改，是吾忧也。"

12. 南宋理宗：赵昀，南宋第五位皇帝，庙号理宗。

13. 濂、洛、关、闽：宋朝理学四个学派。濂指周敦颐，洛指程颐、程颢兄弟，关指张载，闽指朱熹。

14. 巍巍：崇高伟大、高大壮观的样子，形容高大。《论语·泰伯》："巍巍乎！舜禹之有天下也而不与焉。"

◎ 译文

周王室衰微，礼乐制度荒废，导致天下失控。各诸侯之间相互征战，列国伺机争夺政权。

春秋末年，孔子从陬邑出发，感慨各国多遭受不幸，于是四处奔波宣扬礼教。他希望能在乱世间辅佐明君，并且振奋民心。然而当时官室深远，诸侯王不能领悟孔子的良苦用心。更有楚国的狂人接舆唱着歌经过孔子身边，痛骂凤鸟的德行衰退，深切悲叹朝廷的危机，过去的错误已无法挽回，未来的事情还来得及补救，于是孔子回到鲁国，不再外出游历。

对待儒家经典是传承发扬而不是创作新的理论，这不是只讲空话，追溯历史、思考未来，为官吏的公正廉明而编订了《春秋》这部著作，确立最高准则来昭示千秋万代。凤凰不飞来了，黄河中不出现图画，圣人没有出现，担忧这些古代的智慧不能得到充分的传承；我们已经很久不再梦见周公了，伤感距离古代先贤越来越远。所以才会极力倡导仁爱、宽恕、中庸等道理原则，以及约束自己，使自己的言行符合礼制的品德。

孔子在杏坛讲学，天下的士人都来向他请教，就像上万种动物附在麒麟和凤凰的身上一样。其中有颜渊、子路、公冶长、有子、子张、子贡、曾子等七十二位贤人，三千多名学子，目光交汇，充满对知识的渴望。孔子自己说："我小时候生活艰苦，所以学了许多琐碎的技能。"于是诚恳地告诫各位君子，要知道自己担负的责任并长期奋斗，用刚强的意志来自我勉励。世道昏暗不明却用来炫耀，唯独我喜爱古代并勤奋敏捷地求取知识。把富贵看作浮云，思慕有才德的人，听到符合道义的事情就立即去做。不降低自己的志向，不屈辱自己的身份。孔夫子，是集微子、箕子、比干美德和善行于一身的人。世人将孔子看作传授圣贤之道的人，不是没有理由的。颜渊感叹地说："我的老师啊，他的学问道德，抬头仰望，越望越觉得高；努力钻研，越钻研越觉得深。看着好像在前面，忽然又像在后面了。"这是高足弟子对孔子的敬仰之辞，也足以成为千秋万世共同祭祀孔子的人的想法。荆山之玉蕴藏宝贝，幽谷的兰花散发馨香，这是孔子思想无穷无尽的宝藏。

经过了一百多年，孟子从邹国开始宣扬大义，与孔子提倡的仁爱相互辅佐。又过了三百多年，汉武帝推崇儒学，于是有了毛亨、郑玄等人为其解释，董仲舒等人演绎其学说。再过了一千二百多年，南宋理宗朝的濂、洛、关、闽四大学派，勤勉地学习发扬，成就了盛大的景象，并一同在孔庙祭祀。又过了千年，虽然时间一直在流逝，对孔子的赞颂依然美好高尚，来自许多地方的人在孔子门前争相学习，孔学的坚守，在当今社会越来越重要。已建立的孔子学院遍布全球，这是人类文化的

祭孔大典现场　　　　　（图片由济宁日报社提供）

The scene of Confucius Commemoration Ceremony.

奇观。

尽管世事多变，但孔子思想学说却从未衰败过，用"仁者爱人""先欲达人"的思想勉励人们要关爱他人；"己所不欲，勿施于人"的理念则是强调要有尊重他人的高尚节操。团结协作、讲究信用、和睦共处。这些思想足够成为各国之间交往的最高准则，也是各民族和谐相处的宏观策略。孔子的教诲虽然时间久远，但是它们的实践意义却离我们很近，就像寒冬中的松柏一样，历经千万年也不凋谢，这不就是孔子博大胸怀的长远规划和深谋远虑的雄才大略吗？

高耸入云的陵寝，郁郁葱葱的大柏树，云霄万古，黛色参天。抬头仰望这烟雾云霞缭绕的景象，更是增加了心中的敬畏，焚香再次祭拜，愿这美好万古永存。

Text of the Jichou Year (2009) Confucius Commemoration Ceremony

Written by: Fan Zeng

During the declining era of the Zhou Dynasty, proper observance of ritual and music was neglected, and the lands under Heaven lacked guidance. Quibbles between princes led to wars, and vassals sought opportunities to steal the throne.

In the waning years of the end of the Spring and Autumn Period (770 - 481 BCE), Confucius was born in Zouyi (modern-day Qufu). Witnessing the turmoil that many places were suffering, he felt the need to evangelize proper behavior. Facing the troubled times, as the Minister of Ji, Confucius was overzealous. Sequestered deep within his palace, the king knew none of this. Bemoaning the decline of virtue and knowledge, Lu Tong - the Madman of Chu - taught Confucius a valuable lesson. The past cannot be retrieved, but you can still catch up with the future. After Confucius returned to whence he came, ceasing his wandering ways, he endeavored to bring life to his predecessors' doctrines. Chasing the past and thinking about the future, he reflected on his knowledge and wrote the Spring and Autumn Annals to benefit future generations. When the ways of governance are unclear in troubled times, it seems as though the ancient paths have been abandoned; feeling that the God of Dreams no longer gives advice or guidance, the Sage Master was worried about the future. Thus, he advocated the way of benevolence, forgiveness and harmony, and the virtues of self-denial and propriety. After the Apricot Altar was established, the number of scholars who came to learn from him was as numerous as the phoenix's feathers. It was traditionally believed that Confucius had three thousand students, among which 72—including Yanyuan, Zilu, Gongye Chang, Youzi, Zizhang, Zigong, and Zengzi— are most famous. Confucius said he learned many trivial skills when he was young and poor. So he wanted to exhorted sincerelt the true gentleman knows the heavy burden, knows the road is long and has the strength of mind and character to persevere. The world's ambiguity is not an excuse for doing anything other than trying one's best.

Wealth and honor are as insubstantial as clouds; thirst for success is okay, but one could not give up simply because one's thirst has been slaked. Do not lower your ambitions. Do not disgrace yourself. The true Master combines the virtues of Wei Tsze, Kizi, and Bigan. It is not without reason that the world regards the Master's words like a loudly ringing bell. Is it not true that Yanzi said, "As to my teacher's knowledge, you look up, it will be too high to reach; if you drill in, it will be too hard to penetrate; if you look for it in front of you, you will find it behind you?" This disciple's naked admiration shows why the Sage has been worshiped by generation after generation. The endless treasures of Confucianism are its ideas, such as "internal factors being the fundamental reason and external causes the necessary condition."

One hundred years after Confucius, Mencius of Zou complemented his advocacy of benevolence. Three hundred years after Confucius, his words and thoughts were taught by scholars and philosophers such as Master Mao the Senior, Zheng Xuan, and Dong Zhongshu.

When one thousand and two hundred years had passed, Emperor Lizong of the Southern Song Dynasty (1127–1279 CE) encouraged the establishment of the Four Great Schools of Neo-Confucianism and Confucius Temples around the country. Years come and years go. The sun and the moon revolve in the heavens. The words to praise the Master are still sweet upon the ears. The wisdom of Confucius has grown even more famous. Confucius Institutes are located all over the world, and the Master's words have been recognized as a wonder of human culture.

Even as the world changes, the world recognizes the wisdom of Confucianism; the world encourages ideals such as "benevolence is loving others as yourself" and "in order to help yourself, first help others"; and the integral truth of directives such as "be magnanimous and forgiving towards others." Only in harmony can we help each other; only by being trustworthy can we create peace. This can be said to be the ultimate principle of diplomatic relations among all nations. It is also a holistic view of harmony among all ethnic groups. Although this legacy comes from the distant past, it tells wholeheartedly truths that we all experience. Noble integrity, even under duress, is permanent and unfading. Does this ancient approach by the Master seem so far-reaching?

Burning incense in front of the towering mausoleum, surrounded by lush cypress trees, beneath the eternal sky, clouds of smoke rise into the air and increase the awe in my heart. The incense carries my prayers upward to Heaven, and I hope that this moment in time lasts forever.

范曾简介

范　曾：1938年生，江苏南通人，字十翼，中国当代思想家、国学大师、书画家、文学家、诗人。中国美术家协会会员，北京大学中国画法研究院院长、讲席教授，中国艺术研究院博士生导师、研究员，南开大学终身教授、博士生导师，山东大学艺术学院名誉院长。联合国教科文组织"多元文化特别顾问"，英国格拉斯哥大学名誉文学博士，加拿大阿尔伯塔大学荣誉文学博士。曾荣获法国荣誉军团骑士勋章、意大利共和国大将军勋章、首届中华艺文奖终身成就奖。

主要著作：出版有《鲁迅小说插图集》《范曾书画集》《范曾画集》《范曾吟草》《范曾怀抱》《范曾自述》等画集、书法集、诗集、散文集160余部，国家图书馆珍藏其中的130部。擅长人物水墨画，兼长书法、诗文，其作品《灵道歌啸图》等藏于日本冈山范曾美术馆，《八仙图》等藏于中国美术馆，《秋声赋》等藏于美国伯明翰博物馆。

Introduction to Fan Zeng

Fan Zeng, born in 1938 with the courtesy name Shi Yi and the pseudonym Master of Bao Chong zhai, hails from Nantong, Jiangsu Province, China. He is a modern Chinese philosopher, a master of traditional Chinese studies, an accomplished painter and calligrapher, as well as a writer and poet. Currently, he is a member of the Chinese Artists Association, the Director and Chair Professor of the Chinese Painting Research Institute at Peking University, a doctoral supervisor and researcher at the Chinese Academy of Arts, a lifelong professor and doctoral supervisor at Nankai University, and the Honorary Director of the School of Arts at Shandong University. He also serves as a "Special Advisor on Multiculturalism" for UNESCO and holds honorary doctoral degrees from the University of Glasgow in the United Kingdom and the University of Alberta in Canada. Fan Zeng has been awarded the Knight of the Legion of Honor by France, the Grand Cross of the Order of Merit of the Italian Republic, and the Lifetime Achievement Award of the First Chinese Arts and Literature Award.

His major works include over 160 collections of paintings, calligraphy, poetry, and essays, including "Illustrated Collection of Lu Xun's Novels," "Collected Works of Fan Zeng's Calligraphy and Painting," "Fan Zeng's Paintings," "Fan Zeng's Recitations of Grass," "Fan Zeng's Collection of Calligraphy and Painting," "Fan Zeng's Embrace," and "Fan Zeng's Self-Portrait," among others. 130 of these works are preserved in the National Library of China. Fan Zeng excels in figure ink painting, calligraphy, and literary creation. His works such as "Song of the Soul and Dao Singing" are housed in the Fan Zeng Art Museum in Okayama, Japan, "Eight Immortals" in the National Art Museum of China, and "Autumn Sounds Ode" in the Birmingham Museum in the United States.

2010 庚寅年
天下大同　协和万邦

2010, the Year of Gengyin.
The world is a great harmonious family, with all nations living in concord.

纪念孔子诞辰2561年

Commemorating the 2561st Anniversary of Confucius's Birth

庚寅（2010）年祭孔大典祭文

许嘉璐　撰

维公元 2010 年先师孔圣夫子诞日，谨备时蔬玄酒，雅乐升舞，恭奠于大成殿阶下，肃拜追远，上达夫子暨诸先哲先贤。其辞曰：

吾国文明，渊源何远！洪荒无征，蒙昧万年。

既历三皇，五帝相衔；贤哲冥思，归之鬼天。

吾侪[1]何来？终将何还？何者为福？何者为善？

生应何求？何为圣贤？茫茫长夜，踽踽盘桓。

逮及文武，民听达天。周公制礼，明德尚贤。

享祚八百，维系血缘。尾渐不掉，王室东迁。

霸者问鼎，逐鹿中原。强则陵弱，富者欺寒。

悖逆诈伪，淫佚兴乱[2]。岁岁征伐，竟无义战。

呜呼夫子，生悯人寰。少贱多能，屡经磨练。

复礼兴乐，欲挽狂澜。己立立人，孝弟[3]唯先。

修齐治平[4]，悦迩来远。游说列国，不惧厄难。

杏坛论学[5]，大同[6]是盼。人心驱霾，晨曦乍现。

道虽不行，学统绵绵。与时俱进，巨匠迭见。

孟轲弘发，荀卿敷衍。董生继后，道法兼含。

南北一统，合而有辨。孔贾拘守，昌黎呐喊。

迄宋大兴，如日中天。程朱相续，周张并肩[7]。

出入佛道，孔孟真传。人参天地，敬而自反。

天理良心，理学体完。知行合一，世界峰巅。

沉沉浮浮，倏尔千年。伟哉中华，千劫万艰。

百折不挠，国泰民安。环顾全球，熙攘纷乱。

一如春秋，冲突不断。弱肉强食，贪欲泛滥。

嗟我夫子，所述皆验。文明对话，五洲共愿。

2010 年 9 月 28 日，时任山东省委副书记、省政协主席刘伟恭读祭文。（图片由济宁日报社刘项清拍摄）

On September 28th, 2010, Liu Wei, Deputy Secretary of the CPC Shandong Provincial Committee and Chairman of Shandong Provincial Political Consultative Conference at that time, solemnly recited the commemoration text.

仁恕之道，日益播散。促进和睦，中华奉献。
谨此上达，慰我圣贤。伏惟上飨！

◎ 注释

1. 吾侪：我辈；我们这类人。《左传·宣公十一年》："吾侪小人，所谓取诸其怀而与之也。"

2. 悖逆诈伪，淫佚兴乱：违反正道，犯上作乱。《乐记·乐本章》："人化物也者，灭天理而穷人欲者也。于是有悖逆诈伪之心，有淫佚作乱之事。是故强者胁弱，众者暴寡，知者诈愚，勇者苦怯，疾病不养，老幼孤寡不得其所，此大乱之道也。"

3. 孝弟：亦作"孝悌"。《论语·学而》："子曰：'学而时习之，不亦说乎？有朋自远方来，不亦乐乎？人不知而不愠，不亦君子乎？'有子曰：'其为人也孝弟，而好犯上者，鲜矣；不好犯上而好作乱者，未之有也。'"孝，指报答父母的养育之恩；悌，指兄弟姐妹之间的友爱。孝敬父母、尊重爱护兄弟姐妹。孔子非常重视孝悌，认为孝悌是做人、做学问的根本。

4. 修齐治平：修身、齐家、治国、平天下。《礼记·大学》："古之欲明明德于天下者，先治其国；欲治其国者，先齐其家；欲齐其家者，先修其身。"提高自身修为，管理好家庭，治理好国家，安抚天下百姓苍生，泛指伦理哲学（比如齐家的孝，治国的忠，平天下的义）和政治理论。

5. 杏坛论学：杏坛讲学是一个典故，相传孔子当年坐在杏坛上弦歌讲学、教弟子读书。

6. 大同：大同概念出自《礼记·礼运》中的《大道之行也》："大道之行也，天下为公，选贤与能，讲信修睦，故人不独亲其亲，不独子其子，使老有所终，壮有所用，幼有所长，鳏寡孤独废疾者皆有所养；男有分，女有归，货恶其弃于地也，不必藏于己，力恶其不出于身也，不必为己，是故谋闭而不兴，盗窃乱贼而不作，故外户而不闭，是谓大同。"大同是中国古代思想，指人类最终可达到的理想世界，代表着人类对未来社会的美好憧憬。基本特征即为人人友爱互助，家家安居乐业，没有差异，没有战争。

7. 程朱相续，周张并肩：程朱理学是以宋代程颢、程颐、朱熹为代表的一个儒学派别，它强调理性认识和道德实践；周张理学是以周敦颐、张载为代表的一个儒学派别，它强调"无极而太极"的哲学思想，注重对事物本原的探索和认识。

◎ 译文

公元 2010 年先师孔子诞辰之际，我们怀着诚敬的心情备好时令蔬菜、玄酒，弹奏雅乐，表演佾舞。在大成殿的台阶下恭敬地献上祭品，严肃地追忆和祭拜孔子以及众多的先哲先贤。祭文是：

中华文明博大精深，源远流长！混沌初开，文明初始，人类处于蒙昧无知的状态，对世界和自身的认识十分有限，没有留下任何文字记录和历史记载。三皇五帝时期，各个部落逐渐融合，古代的先哲开始探索自然，探求规律，并将这种思考归结于"鬼天"（可能指代某种超自然的力量或规律）。人类从何处来？生命的起源和本质是什么？生命的归宿和终结又在何处？什么是幸福，什么是善良？在人生中追求什么才是真正的价值和意义？什么样的人才可以称之为圣贤？人生的道路何其漫长，如同在墨色长夜中踽踽独行，孤独探索。

到了周文王和周武王时期，周公旦制定了礼乐制度，民众的听闻在这一时期达到了顶峰。在礼乐制度的影响下，逐渐注重对人的品德和才能的培养，明确了道德标准，推崇贤能之人。依靠宗法制度，周王朝的统治延续了近八百年，而随着分封制的不断发展，诸侯割据，势力渐起，周王朝日渐式微，公元前770年，周王朝将都城东迁移至洛邑。强大的诸侯国开始崛起，各国实力此消彼长，称霸天下的野心和欲望逐渐膨胀。诸侯攻伐、生灵涂炭，强国欺压弱国，强者压迫弱者，有钱有势的人欺凌贫困饥寒的人。社会动荡、礼崩乐坏，悖逆俗矩、虚伪欺诈、淫乱奢侈、犯上作乱的现象屡见不鲜，年年征战，却没有正义的战争，社会长期处于持续的冲突和动荡之中。

夫子啊！你生在人间却怜悯人间。出身苦寒却身负才能，屡经挫折，终得大成。你恢复礼乐制度，挽救狂澜；你主张自立立人，孝悌为先；你主张修齐治平，使远方的人欣慕而来；你游说列国，不惧怕困难和厄运；你在杏坛论学讲经，期盼天下大同；你拨开人心中的迷雾，像晨曦一样照亮了黑暗。虽然你的思想在当时没有得到广泛的实施和接受，但你的学说却历代相传，延续至今。随着时代的发展，涌现出许多杰出的思想家和教育家，孟子阐发你的学说，荀子传播你的思想，董仲舒继承了你的学说后，又兼容并包道家和法家的思想。南北朝时期，中国实现了南北方统一，儒家思想得到进一步发展和传播，但因地理、历史和文化背景的差异，南方儒家更注重实践和具体应用，北方儒家更注重学术和经典文化研究，两者和而不同，碰撞融合。孔颖达、贾公彦等儒学大家坚守传统礼教，继承并发扬传统儒学精髓；韩愈主张以文载道，倡导古文运动，抨击时弊，呐喊社会正义。衍至宋朝，儒家思想得到进一步发展和传承，逐渐成为中国传统文化的主流思想。在这一时期，程朱理学和周张理学并立，互相竞争但也互相借鉴，他们的传承和发展，使得儒家思想更加丰富和深入。儒家学者们在传承儒家文化的同时，也借鉴了佛家和道家的思想，通过吸收佛、道思想，进一步丰富了儒家文化的内涵，使得儒家思想更加具有时代性和现实性。他们认为，人是天地之间的中心，人的行为和道德应该符合天地的规律和自然的法则。同时，人们也应该通过自我反省和反思，不断修正自己的行为和思想，以达到更高的境界。他们主张遵循天理良心，以道德规范作为自己的行为准则，强调通过内在的修养和外在的实践达到完善个人和社会的目的，同时主张知行合一，强调知识和实践结合，认为只有通过知行合一才能实现人类社会的完美和谐。

中华文明历经沉浮，斗转星移已逾千年。伟大的中华！经历了无数劫难与艰辛，但仍百折不挠、坚韧不拔地发展下去，始终保持着国家的繁荣和人民的安宁。现在我们环顾全球，国际社会纷杂混乱，一如春秋战国时期的诸侯争霸冲突不断。弱肉强食的规则仍在继续，贪欲泛滥成灾。啊！夫子啊，你所讲述的道理在今天依然适用，进行文明对话是全球共同的期盼。你所倡导的"仁恕之道"的价值观正在日益传播和推广，促进了世界各国的和睦相处和共同发展，为世界各国之间的交流和合作提供了中国智慧。在此我谨向您表达诚挚的敬意和感激之情！

伏请您享用供品！

祭孔大典现场　　　　　　　　　　　　（图片由济宁日报社提供）

The scene of Confucius Commemoration Ceremony.

Text of the Gengyin Year (2010) Confucius Commemoration Ceremony

Written by: Xu Jialu

In the year 2010, on the Gregorian Calendar, today is the birthday of our departed Master Confucius. Now is the time to prepare the wine. Now is the time for elegant music and dance. Now is the time for a memorial ceremony at the steps of Dacheng Hall. Genuflecting, I devoutly offer sacrifice to the departed Master and all the sages.

As it is written:

How far back can our country's civilization be traced? From prehistoric times to the invention of pottery, writing, and metalworking.

As the obscuring mists of time grow thinner, the Three Sovereigns and Five Emperors appeared; deep in meditation, the ancients began to explore the laws of Heaven and mankind.

Where do we come from? Where are we going? What are blessings? What is good?

What should one seek in life? What is a sage? Even with wisdom lighting the way, life's long road is both dark and uncertain.

Seeking both civil and military success requires listening to the mandate of Heaven. The Duke of Zhou established the concepts of etiquette and showed clear respect for the virtuous.

As a result, the dynasty of his heirs lasted for 800 years. However, as the kings of Zhou were subverted by their underlings, they were forced to move eastwards.

Attempting to seize political power, the warlords competed for the Central Plains. The strong and wealthy oppressed the weak and hungry.

Disobedience and hypocrisy led to chaos. Year in and year out, the troops were mobilized for wars that had no just cause.

Preaching compassion to the quotidian world, the humble yet talented young man who would become the Great Sage was challenged again and again.

Reviving the proper observance of ritual and music, he helped turn back the tide of dissolution and inertia. To improve others, one must first improve oneself. Improving oneself begins with filial piety.

Cultivate the self, manage your family and country well, and appease the common people's aspirations in the world; this is good news that will spread both far and wide. Roaming throughout the land, he had no fear of adversity or hardship.

Preaching the hopes of Great Harmony from the Apricot Altar, he helped clear away the fog in people's hearts and illuminated the darkness like the rising sun at dawn.

Trying is a prerequisite for succeeding, and academic traditions follow one after another. In accordance with the pace of the times, new sages came on the scene.

Mencius, who inherited and developed these teaching; Xunzi, who synthesized and revised them. Then, Dong Zhongshu integrated the cosmology of yin and yang into Confucianism.

Even as the North and the South were unified, they could still maintain their distinctions. Kong Yingda revised, and Han Yu advocated.

As the Song Dynasty flourished, Confucianism was as bright as the sun at high noon. The Rationalistic School of Cheng Yi, Cheng Hao, and Zhu Xi led to Zhou Dunyi and Zhang Zai explaining the relationship between human conduct and universal forces.

Integrating with Buddhism and Daoism, the words and traditions of Confucius and Mencius were passed down. Respect man's unity with Heaven and Earth.

The heavenly principles of conscience and science are complete. Unity of knowledge and action leads to the best developments.

Rising and falling over thousands of years, China is still a great country despite its many hardships.

Perseverance of will leads to a peaceful country and safety for the people. Looking at today's world, everything is topsy-turvy.

Just like the Spring and Autumn Period, there are continuous conflicts erupting. The law of the jungle reigns supreme, and greed is rampant.

Alas, my Master, everything I have said has been verified. Dialogue among civilizations is the common aspiration of all five continents.

The way of kindness and forgiveness is spreading day by day. China contributes to the promotion of loving-kindness.

Solemnly and respectfully so I do say to the Sage as I respectfully beseech you!

许嘉璐简介

　　许嘉璐：1937 年 6 月生，江苏淮安人，字若石，民进会员。中国著名语言学家、教育家、社会活动家。现任北京师范大学人文宗教高等研究院、中国文化院院长。第七届、第八届全国人大代表，全国人大常委会委员，全国人大教育科学文化卫生委员会委员，第九届全国人大常委会副委员长。中华炎黄文化研究会会长，北京师范大学人文宗教高等研究院院长、汉语文化学院院长，尼山论坛组委会主席。

　　研究领域：古代汉语、训诂学、音韵学、《说文》学、古代文化学。

　　主要著作：出版或发表《古代文体常识》《中国古代衣食住行》《古语趣谈》《未辍集》《未成集》《未了集》《语言文字学及其应用研究》等多部专著及大量学术论文。主编《中国传统语言学辞典》《中国古代礼俗辞典》《古代汉语》《语言文字应用研究丛书》和《古今字汇释》等。主持《文白对照十三经》《文白对照诸子集成》《二十四史全译》等大型文化工程。

Introduction to Xu Jialu

Xu Jialu, born in June 1937 in Huaian, Jiangsu Province, is a prominent Chinese linguist, educator, and social activist. He is currently serving as the President of the Institute for Advanced Studies in Humanities and Religion at Beijing Normal University and the Chinese Culture Institute. He has also held positions as a member of the 7th and 8th National People's Congress, a member of the Standing Committee of the National People's Congress, a member of the Education, Science, Culture and Health Committee of the National People's Congress, and the Vice Chairman of the Standing Committee of the 9th National People's Congress. Additionally, he is the President of the Chinese Culture Research Association, the Dean of the Institute for Advanced Studies in Humanities and Religion at Beijing Normal University, the Dean of the Han Language and Culture College, and the Chairman of the Nishan Forum Organizing Committee.

His research focuses on Ancient Chinese, philology, phonology, Shuowen Jiezi studies, and Ancient Culture.

His major works include "Common Knowledge of Ancient Literary Styles," "Daily Life in Ancient China," "Fun Talks on Ancient Expressions," "Collections of Unfinished Works," "Studies on Linguistics and its Applications," and many academic papers. He has also edited "Dictionary of Traditional Chinese Linguistics," "Dictionary of Ancient Chinese Customs," "Ancient Chinese," "Series on Research on Language and Writing Applications," and "Explanations of Ancient and Modern Characters." He has led large-scale cultural projects such as the "Thirteen Classics in Comparison of Text and White" and "Complete Translation of the Twenty-Four Histories."

2011 辛卯年

儒济天下　和宁四方

2011, the Year of Xinmao.
Confucianism benefits the world, bringing peace to all corners.

纪念孔子诞辰
2562 年

Commemorating the 2562nd Anniversary of Confucius's Birth

辛卯（2011）年祭孔大典祭文

杨朝明　撰

维公元 2011 年 9 月 28 日，岁在辛卯，至圣先师孔子诞辰 2562 周年，山东各界人士、港澳台同胞、海内外宾朋，谨备蔬果鲜花，献以乐舞，敬告夫子之圣灵。

煌煌中华，郁郁[1]文明，
唐虞稽古，夏商乂宁。
文武周公，天下景从。[2]
嗟我夫子，降诞昌平[3]。
少贱鄙事，博学多能。[4]
通天之德，旁彻物情，[5]
金声玉振，爰集大成。[6]

乾坤并立，日月代明[7]，
阴阳合和，万物蒸蒸。
首出庶物，人为秀灵[8]。
礼自外作，乐由心生。[9]
好恶有节，敬德怀刑。[10]

言则忠信，行则笃敬。[11]
和而不流，与时偕行！

为政以德，仁爱百姓。
举直措枉，尚贤使能。
知民之欲，察民之情，[12]
富而后教，德化流行。
远来近悦，万邦咸宁。

大哉夫子，既圣且明，
出类拔萃，卓乎独盛。
垂仪立极，百代同宗。[13]
三千弟子，惟道是弘。
章句汉唐，义理宋明。[14]
远播欧美，泽及亚东，
夫子精华，代代相承。

秋高气爽，玉宇澄清，
社会祥和，物阜民丰。
巍巍神州，荡荡[15]德风，
仁爱诚信，中华魂灵。
济济多士[16]，众志成城：
融古铸今，中西会通，
而今而后，乃昌乃隆。

炎黄子孙，祈祥鞠躬：
四海一家，天下大同！
伏惟尚飨！

2011 年 9 月 28 日，时任山东省委副书记、省政协
主席刘伟恭读祭文。（图片由济宁日报社刘项清拍摄）

On September 28th, 2011, Liu Wei, Deputy Secretary of the CPC
Shandong Provincial Committee and Chairman of Shandong
Provincial Political Consultative Conference at that time, solemnly
recited the commemoration text.

◎ 注释

1. 郁郁：文化繁盛的样子。《论语·八佾》："周监于二代，郁郁乎文哉！"

2. 唐虞稽古，夏商乂宁。文武周公，天下景从：唐虞，指唐尧虞舜。《书·周官》："唐虞稽古，建官惟百……夏商官倍，亦克用乂。"按《尧典》《舜典》开头，均为"曰若稽古……"。意指唐尧、虞舜之事是由口耳相传而来，属传说。乂宁，治理，安宁。此四句指出由唐虞而夏商，由夏商而西周，特别是文武周公时期，政治文明逐次演进，文化影响也日渐扩大。

3. 降诞昌平：诞，降生，诞生。昌平，在今曲阜市东南。《史记·孔子世家》："孔子生于鲁昌平乡陬邑。"

4. 少贱鄙事，博学多能：鄙事，指低贱而琐碎的事务。孔子自称："吾少也贱，故多能鄙事。"但其弟子子贡却认为："固天纵之将圣，又多能也。"应将两者结合起来理解。

5. 通天之德，旁彻物情：《易·系辞下》："庖牺氏之王天下也，仰观象于天，俯观法于地，观鸟兽之文与地之宜，近取诸身，远取诸物，于是始作八卦，以通神明之德，以类万物之情。"孔子集成上古三代之学，更兼具三代圣王之德，故此是借指孔子之德能。

6. 金声玉振，爰集大成：《孟子·万章下》："孔子之谓集大成。集大成也者，金声而玉振之也。金声也者，始条理也；

玉振之也者，终条理也。"

7. 日月代明：《礼记·中庸》："仲尼祖述尧舜，宪章文武……辟如四时之错行，如日月之代明。"祭文取义于此。

8. 人为秀灵：出自《孔子家语·礼运》，原作："人者，天地之德，阴阳之交，鬼神之会，五行之秀。"

9. 礼自外作，乐由心生：《礼记·乐记》，原作："乐由中出，礼自外作。"意为乐由内心发出，礼则为外在约束及表现。

10. 好恶有节，敬德怀刑：《礼记·乐记》："好恶无节于内，知诱于外，不能反躬，天理灭矣。"《论语·里仁》："君子怀德，小人怀土；君子怀刑，小人怀惠。"《说文》："怀，思念也。"此指人注意力所集中的地方，有关注之意。刑：宋张有《复古编》曰："从刀井，法也。"字形与汉石经一致。今本皆作"刑"，有法典、礼法之义。实际上，此"刑"与"型"相通，有法式、典范、榜样的意义。如《大盂鼎铭》中"今我唯即型宪于文王正德"，《诗·周颂·我将》中"仪式刑文王之典，日靖四方"，《诗·大雅·思齐》中"刑于寡妻，至于兄弟，以御于家邦"，皆有此意。祭文此处意为心有典范、法则。

11. 言则忠信，行则笃敬：《论语·卫灵公》，原作："言忠信，行笃敬，虽蛮貊之邦行矣。"笃敬，忠厚恭敬。

12. 知民之欲，察民之情：《孔子家语·入官》："君子莅民，不可以不知民之性而达诸民之情。既知其性，又习其情，然后民乃从命矣。"祭文二句取义于此。

13. 出类拔萃，卓乎独盛。垂仪立极，百代同宗：仪、极，皆指法则、法度。如曲阜孔庙大成门旁悬雍正御书对联："先觉先知为万古伦常立极；至诚至圣与两间功化同流。"《孟子·公孙丑上》："麒麟之于走兽，凤凰之于飞鸟，泰山之于丘垤，河海之于行潦，类也。圣人之于民，亦类也。出于其类，拔乎其萃，自生民以来，未有盛于孔子也。"进而指出，自有人类以来，就没有比孔子还要伟大的。

14. 章句汉唐，义理宋明：此指儒学尤其是经学发展的两个阶段。一般说来，汉至唐比较重视章句、训诂之学，而宋至明则比较重视经义、义理之学。

15. 荡荡：广大的样子。

16. 济济多士：济济，众多的样子；多士，古指众多的贤士，也指百官。

◎ **译文**

公元 2011 年 9 月 28 日，时值辛卯年，至圣先师孔子诞辰 2562 周年。山东各界人士、港澳台同胞、海内外宾朋，恭敬地备好蔬果鲜花、雅乐佾舞，告慰先师孔子的圣灵。

伟大的中华文明，辉煌且灿烂。从唐尧虞舜到夏商西周，特别是文武周公时期，政治文明逐次演进，文化影响也日渐扩大。我的夫子啊！降生在昌平，小时候生活艰难学会了很多生存的技艺，后来通过勤奋学习，掌握了广博的知识和多种技能。他有通达天地的美德，又有洞悉世间万物的性情。他知识渊博，才学精到，集成上古三代之学，更兼具三代圣王之德。

天地乾坤并立，日月交替辉映，阴阳和谐，万物繁荣昌盛。世间万物周而复始，人是其中最为优秀的存在。礼是由外部逐渐形成的，它规范人的行为，使得人们更好地适应社会；乐则是由内心所产生的，它能够表达人们内心的情感与感受，增强人与人之间的信任和联系。人应敬重道德，敬畏刑律而严守法纪。对于好的事物应该向往和推崇，对于不好的事物则应远离和抵制。说话忠诚守信，做事厚道谨慎。既要保持和谐，又要不失个性，既要紧跟时代步伐，又要不断更新知识和观念，适应时代的需求。

为政者应当以德行来治理国家，关心和爱护百姓，选拔正直无私的人，纠正邪恶不正的人，重视贤能的人并给予他们发挥才能的机会。为政者要深入基层，关注百姓的诉求，了解社会实际情况，在人民富裕之后再进行教育，通过道德教化，使得美好的风尚在社会中广泛流行。先让国内的人民欢悦无怨，于是远处的人就会慕名而来投奔，这样国家才会安宁太平。

啊！伟大的孔子！你圣明而智慧，超越常人，卓越无比。你树立了做人的规范和标准，被后世子孙共同尊崇，流芳百世。弟子三千，在你的教诲下秉持道义，弘扬真理。汉唐时期注重章句、训诂之学，宋明时期则比较重视经义、义理之学。这些思想不仅在中国流传，还远播欧美及东亚地区，被世界各地的人们所传承和发扬，你的智慧也因此得以代代相传。

仲秋时节，晴空万里，天气凉爽，天空清澈而透明。社会安定祥和，物质丰富，人民生活富裕。伟大的中华大地，道德之风高尚且纯正，讲仁爱、重诚信成为人民的基本遵循，这是中华文明的灵魂所在。人才济济，万众一心：融合古文化，铸就今文明，中西文化交流融合，从今以后，中华文明将会更加繁荣昌盛！作为炎黄子孙，我们怀揣着敬畏的心情祈求祥瑞降临：四海之内皆为一家，天下为公，社会大同！

伏请您享用供品！

祭孔大典现场　　　　　　　（图片由济宁日报社提供）

The scene of Confucius Commemoration Ceremony.

Text of the Xinmao Year (2011) Confucius Commemoration Ceremony

Written by: Yang Chaoming

On the Gregorian Calendar, today is September 28, 2011. On the Chinese Lunar Calendar, it is the year of the Gold Rabbit. Two thousand, five hundred and sixty-two years have passed since the birth of our Master Confucius. Now, people from all over Shandong, compatriots from Hong Kong, Macao, and Taiwan, and domestic and international guests and friends have prepared offerings of fruits and flowers and offerings of music and dance to honor the Master's holy spirit.

From the mythical Emperors Yao and Shun to the shining years of the Xia and the Shang dynasties, the brilliant land of China has had a glorious legacy of civilization and style.

The governmental ideals inherited by the Duke of Zhou have spread throughout all the lands under Heaven. The Great Master was born in Changping.

Despite humble origins and a lack of money, he was erudite, versatile, and rich in talent. A virtuoso born of Heaven, he had a deep understanding of human emotion and worldly concerns; he showed profound knowledge, the ability to learn well, and the ability to combine the advantages of several generations into greatness.

The sky and Earth are illuminated by the sun and moon. Yin and yang are in balance, and all things flourish.

With human beings the greatest among them, all things in the world experience coming and going, alpha and omega. Rituals are an external display of the joy which comes from the heart.

People should respect morality, bear in mind the punishments meted out by the law, yearn for and admire good things, and stay away from and resist bad things. Be faithful with your words and respectful with your deeds.

Refrain from blindly pursuing harmony; adhere instead to moral principles, and keep pace with the changing times!

Govern with virtue and morality and love the people. Appoint upright officials, remove crooked ones, respect the virtuous, and use the talented.

Withe the governor knowing the people's desires and observing their sentiments, prosperity for the people is the prerequisite to further educating them; through moral education, good behavior can spread throughout society.

That all nations can achieve peace is good news that will be spread both far and wide.

Great Master, you are both holy and wise. Exceptional. Glorious. You stand out from the crowd.

You established norms and standards for upright behavior that have been respected for a hundred generations and will be respected for hundreds of generations. Your three thousand disciples upheld morality and promoted the truth.

Chapters and sentences from the Han and Tang dynasties, principles from the Song and Ming dynasties. The essence of the Master has been passed down from generation to generation. It has spread as far as all parts of Asia, as far as Europe, and as far as the United States.

As the land experiences the fresh and pure autumn weather, society has peace, and the people are prosperous.

The land of China is majestic and imposing, the sages' virtues have spread throughout the whole land, and the spirit of the Chinese people is one of benevolence and integrity.

United with the great scholars, we have an indomitable unity of will: integrating with the past and becoming one with the present, China and the West are connected, and both the present and the future will be prosperous.

Descendants of a time before time, bow your heads and bodies in prayer and supplication: in search of the Great Harmony, let all people under Heaven be as one family! I respectfully beseech you!

杨朝明简介

杨朝明：1962 年生，山东梁山人，历史学博士。山东大学儒学高等研究院教授，博士生导师。国际儒学联合会副理事长，中华孔子学会副会长，尼山世界儒学中心学术委员，中国哲学史学会常务理事等。历任《齐鲁学刊》编辑，曲阜师范大学孔子文化学院院长和历史文化学院院长，尼山世界儒学中心副主任，孔子研究院院长。第十四届全国人大代表，第十三届全国政协委员，山东省决策咨询委员会特聘专家。

研究领域：主要从事中国古代文明和传统文化研究、孔子儒学与早期典籍研究。

主要著作：《鲁文化史》《周公事迹研究》《儒家文献与儒家学术研究》《出土文献与早期儒学研究》《孔子事迹编年会按》《论语诠解》《孔子家语通解》《孔孟正源》《〈孔子家语〉综合研究》《孔子之道与中国信仰》《中华传统八德诠解》《儒学精神与中国梦》《孔子的叮咛》《从文化自知到文化自信》《孔子文化与当代中国》《让儒学温暖世界》《国学通识课》《至圣孔子》等。

Introduction to Yang Chaoming

Yang Chaoming, born in 1962 in Liangshan, Shandong Province, holds a Ph.D. in History. He is a professor and doctoral supervisor at the Institute of Confucian Studies at Shandong University. He also holds positions as Vice Chairman of the International Confucian Association, Vice President of the Chinese Confucius Society, Academic Committee Member of the Nishan World Confucianism Center, and Executive Director of the Chinese Society for the History of Philosophy. He has held various roles including editor of "Qilu Academic Journal," Dean of the Confucius Culture Institute and the School of History and Culture at Qufu Normal University, Vice Director of the Nishan World Confucianism Center, and President of the Confucius Research Institute. He has served as a delegate to the 14th National People's Congress, a member of the 13th National Committee of the Chinese People's Political Consultative Conference, and a specially appointed expert of the Decision-making Consultative Committee of Shandong Province.

His research primarily focuses on ancient Chinese civilization and traditional culture, as well as Confucianism and ancient classics.

His major works include "History of Lu Culture," "Study of the Deeds of Duke Zhou," "Research on Confucian Literature and Academic Studies," "Research on Excavated Documents and Early Confucianism," "Chronological Compilation of Confucius's Deeds," "Interpretation of the Analects," "Comprehensive Interpretation of the Family Sayings of Confucius," "Source of Confucius and Mencius," "Comprehensive Study of the Family Sayings of Confucius," "Confucius's Way and Chinese Beliefs," "Interpretation of Eight Virtues of Chinese

Tradition," "Spirit of Confucianism and Chinese Dream," "Confucius's Exhortations," "From Cultural Self-awareness to Cultural Confidence," "Confucius Culture and Contemporary China," "Let Confucianism Warm the World," "General Course of National Studies," "The Sage Confucius," etc.

2012 壬辰年
文化圣地　共有家园

2012, the Year of Renchen.
A cultural sanctuary, a common homeland.

纪念孔子诞辰

2563 年

Commemorating the 2563rd Anniversary of Confucius's Birth

壬辰（2012）年祭孔大典祭文

董金裕　撰

维公元 2012 年 9 月 28 日，欣逢孔圣 2563 年诞辰纪念，我中华各族群同胞，以及国际嘉宾良朋，缅怀盛德伟业，以虔诚之心、景仰之情，谨备鲜花美果、佾舞雅乐，敬献于孔庙大成殿暨两庑，告祭大成至圣先师与夫诸圣哲贤儒。其辞曰：

天地设位，人在其中。天行刚健，地道宽弘。
品物流形[1]，化育功隆。人禀五常，灵秀所钟。
法天之德，效地之用。[2]赞之参之，与之同功。

唯我夫子，博通世务。上应天时，下顺风土。[3]
远宗尧舜，近法文武。删述六经[4]，以教生徒。
循序而进，孜孜矻矻[5]。成德达材，栽培无数。

仁道思想，众德汇涵。明德亲民，止于至善。[6]
推己及人，是为其方。礼以行之，益加发扬。
华夏文明，赖以发皇。驯致大同，协和万邦。[7]

与时俱进，弥足珍贵。集圣大成，出类拔萃。
其所成就，卓越崔巍。典型既在，吾谁与归？
万民景从，仰承教诲。千秋万世，永蒙遗徽。

恭逢圣诞，我心欢畅。秉持诚意，其喜洋洋。
载歌载舞，俎豆馨香。奉承而进，伏惟尚飨。
护佑生灵，教化其昌。乐道好礼，同沐祯祥。

2012 年 9 月 28 日，时任山东省委常委、副省长孙伟恭读祭文。 （图片由济宁日报社刘项清拍摄）

On September 28th, 2012, Sun Wei, Member of the Standing Committee of the CPC Shandong Provincial Committee and Vice Governor of Shandong Province at that time, solemnly recited the commemoration text.

◎ 注释

1. 品物流形：品物，万物。流，赋予。意思是万物孕育形态，也可以理解为各种各样事物。《易象》："大哉乾元，万物资始，乃统天。云行雨施，品物流形。"

2. 法天之德，效地之用：《道德经》："人法地，地法天，天法道，道法自然。"要求人应效法天地之德性，遵守事物之内在法则，摒弃妄念，清心寡欲，顺应自然，宠辱不惊。

3. 上应天时，下顺风土：这句话表达了顺应天地自然的哲学思想，强调了人与自然的和谐共生关系。"上应天时"是指要顺应天意，即顺应自然规律和宇宙的运行规律。提醒人们要认识到自然的力量和不可抗拒性，不要试图逆天而行，而是要顺应天意，尊重自然规律。"下顺风土"是指要顺应地理环境，即考虑当地的气候、土壤、水资源等因素，因地制宜地进行生产和生活活动。提醒人们要认识到地理环境的重要性，尊重当地的自然条件和文化传统，合理利用资源，保护环境。

4. 删述六经："删述"是指删减述作，即对古代文献进行删减和整理，以便更好地传承和教授。这里的"六经"指的是中国古代的六部经典著作，包括《诗》《书》《礼》《易》《乐》《春秋》。孔子博物馆藏有孔子《删述六经图》，画面上方有文及赞，曰："哀公十四年丁巳，孔子年六十八，季康子使人迎孔子。孔子归鲁，然鲁终不用孔子，孔子亦不求仕，乃叙《书》、传《礼记》、删《诗》、正《乐》、序《易》象、系、象、说卦、文言，弟子盖三千焉，身通六艺者七十二人。"赞曰："辙环天下，到不可行。曰归乎来，修我典刑。三千其徒，七十高弟。删述六经，垂宪万世。"

5. 孜孜矻矻：形容勤勉不懈怠的样子。唐·韩愈《争臣论》："自古圣人贤士皆非有求于闻用也，闵其时之不平，人之不义，得其道，不敢独善其身，而必以廉济天下也，孜孜矻矻，死而后已。"

6. 明德亲民，止于至善：大学的宗旨，在于彰显光明的品德；在于反省提高自己的道德并推己及人，使人人都能改过自新、弃恶从善；在于让整个社会都能达到完美的道德之境并长久地保持下去。《大学》："大学之道，在明明德，在亲民，在止于至善。"

7. 协和万邦：《书·虞书·尧典》："克明俊德，以亲九族；九族既睦，平章百姓；百姓昭明，协和万邦。"

◎ 译文

公元 2012 年 9 月 28 日，是孔子诞辰 2563 年。中华名族群同胞及世界各地的朋友会聚于此，怀揣着虔诚的心情，带着深深的敬仰之意，准备鲜花美果、佾舞雅乐，恭敬地供奉在孔庙大成殿及两庑，以告祭大成至圣先师孔子及诸位圣哲贤儒。祭文是：

天与地有自然的界限和定位，人类生活在自然之中，遵循自然的规律，顺应天地之道。天的运行刚健有力，地的形态广大无边。万物在自然中流动变化孕育形体，化育出伟大的功绩。人天生具备仁、义、礼、智、信五常之德，是天赋灵性和智慧的集中体现，应效法天地之德性，遵守事物之内在法则，赞美天地自然的伟大之处，并学习尊重自然规律，实现人与自然和谐共生。

只有我们夫子，他博学多才，通晓世间事物，在上顺应天意，在下顺应地理。推崇尧舜的治国理念和文王、武王的治国方式。他删减述作，整理六经，以传道授业为己任，通过循序渐进的教学方式，孜孜不倦地培养学生，使他们成为有德行、有才能的人，这种教育方式为当时社会培养了无数人才，同时也对后世产生了深远影响。

仁道思想涵盖了各种美德和道德规范，反省提高自己的道德并推己及人，能够使人弃旧图新，整个社会都能达到完美的道德之境并长久地保持下去。推己及人、将心比心是实现互相理解的方法，用礼来规范自己的言行，并不断发扬光大。华夏文明得以弘扬传承，各个国家、各个民族和谐共生，逐渐实现大同之世。

孔子思想与时俱进，弥足珍贵，汇集众多先贤圣哲的智慧和成就，出类拔萃。你的成就卓越非常，就像崔巍的山峰一样高大雄伟，你是万世之楷模，我们应当争相效仿。万民心悦诚服地追随，敬仰并聆听教诲。千秋万世，永远承蒙孔子遗留下的宝贵思想。

敬逢孔子诞辰，我的心中充满喜悦之情。秉持着真诚和敬仰之情，内心充满喜悦和快乐，奏响雅乐，佾舞飞扬，祭祀的礼器散发出馨香。恭敬地向孔子献上祭品，请享用这微薄的祭品。请庇护这世间的生灵，让孔子思想在这世间繁荣兴盛，人人乐于行善，追求道德，重礼用礼，共同享受吉祥和幸福的生活。

祭孔大典现场　　　　　　　（图片由济宁日报社提供）

The scene of Confucius Commemoration Ceremony.

Text of the Renchen Year (2012) Confucius Commemoration Ceremony

Written by: Tung Chin-yue

On the Gregorian Calendar, today is September 28, 2012. Two thousand, five hundred and sixty-three years have passed since Confucius's birth. Compatriots from all of China's ethnic groups and friends from foreign countries have gathered to pay homage to his great achievements. People with pious hearts and great admiration for our departed Sage have prepared flowers and fruits, dance and music, and come to the Dacheng Hall in Qufu's Confucius Temple to offer sacrifices to the heavenly Sage, to the ancestors and all the saints, philosophers, and scholars.

As it is written:

When Heaven and Earth were established, humans were among that which was created. The movement of the celestial bodies is vigorous, and the principles of the Earth are firm.

Change and metamorphosis are vital for education, cultivation, and improvement. Smart and beautiful people are endowed with the five virtues.

The virtues of law and Heaven are also the virtues of Earth and man. Praise them, participate in them, and succeed with them.

Our great Master was knowledgeable in world affairs. The things of Heaven's realm are Heaven's responsibility. The things of Earth's realm are mankind's responsibility.

Building on the tradition of the mythical emperors Yao and Shun, he created laws and cultural practices. Editing and compiling the Six Classics, he taught them to his disciples.

Diligently advancing step by step. Achieving virtue. Achieving ethical awareness. Cultivating disciples beyond counting.

The ideology of benevolence and morality came about from the convergence of virtues. Be virtuous and close to the people's will, and strive for perfection.

Respecting oneself and others is the only correct way. Treating others with courtesy improves your moral character.

Open-mindedness is a prerequisite of Chinese civilization. In this way, the Great Harmony will be brought about for all nations.

There is enormous value in moving forward in accordance with the times. Each era and dynasty has recognized the outstanding nature of Confucianism and produced their own studies of it.

Magnificent, outstanding, and splendid, mere words are not enough to express the greatness. Following these models makes it easier to find the numberless like-minded persons who also follow him and admire his teachings. For a thousand times a thousand autumns, his legacy will last.

In congratulating the anniversary of the birth of the Great Sage, my heart is filled with joy. I am sincere in my joy.

I present offerings of song, offerings of dance, and offerings of fragrant incense burned in ritual vessels. With these words of welcome and praise, I respectfully beseech you!

I ask you to offer your protection to all living things, to offer them education, and to help them prosper. And may those who follow the good examples of ritual and etiquette jointly experience good fortune.

董金裕简介

董金裕：1945 年生，台湾省苗栗县人，知名学者、儒学研究专家。现任台湾政治大学名誉教授、国际儒学联合会副理事长。曾任静宜女子文理学院中文系教授兼系主任，台湾政治大学中文系系主任、文学院院长、教务长，第一、二届国际道家学术大会代表人，东海大学中文研究所兼任教授，中兴大学中文系兼任教授，编译馆国中国文教科书编辑小组召集人、中国文化基本教材编辑小组召集人、国立编译馆高中国文教科书编辑小组委员。

研究领域：理学、儒学、经学。

主要著作：《章实斋学记》《宋永嘉学派之学术思想》《宋儒风范》《正气文选析》《忠臣孝子的悲愿——明夷待访录》《怀旧布新集》《至圣先师孔子释奠解说》《朱熹学术考论》《周濂溪集今注今译》等专著及百余篇学术论文。

Introduction to Tung Chin-yue

Tung Chin-yue, born in 1945 in Miaoli County, Taiwan Province, is a renowned scholar and expert in Confucian studies. Currently, he holds the position of Honorary Professor at National Chengchi University and Vice President of the International Confucian Association. He also serves as a professor and department chair at Providence University's Department of Chinese Literature. Previously, Tung Chin-yue held various academic positions, including Department Chair and Dean of the College of Liberal Arts at National Chengchi University, as well as Director of Academic Affairs. He has represented Taiwan at the First and Second International Daoist Academic Conferences and has served as a visiting professor at Donghai University's Institute of Chinese Studies and as an adjunct professor in the Department of Chinese Literature at Chung Hsing University. Additionally, he has held positions such as professor, department chair, and dean at National Chengchi University.

His research interests primarily focus on Neo-Confucianism, Confucianism, and classical Chinese studies.

His major works include: "Records of Zhangshizhai's Learning," "Academic Thoughts of the Song-Yongjia School," "Exemplary Virtues of the Song Confucians," "Analysis of Selected Works of Zhengqi," "The Sorrowful Aspirations of Loyal Officials and Filial Sons: Records of Mingyi's Awaited Visit," "Collection of Nostalgic Reflections and New Ideas," "Interpretation of Confucius's Ritual Offerings to the Most Holy Teacher," "Studies on Zhu Xi's Academic Thoughts," and "Annotations and Translations of the Collection of Zhou Lianxi." He has authored numerous monographs and over a hundred academic papers.

2013 癸巳年
文化凝聚正能量
同心共筑中国梦

2013, the Year of Guisi.
Cultural cohesion gathers positive energy, jointly building
the Chinese dream.

纪念孔子诞辰
2564
年

Commemorating the 2564th Anniversary of Confucius's Birth

癸巳（2013）年祭孔大典祭文

彭　林　撰

惟夏历癸巳之年，辛酉之月，日在丁酉，恭逢大成至圣先师孔子诞辰 2564 年，山东省人民政府敬以释奠大典、鲜花雅乐之奉，祗告圣灵曰：

伟哉夫子，如岳之耸。德尊道隆，海内归宗。
多士肃肃，庙堂雍雍。典祀有常，是仰是崇。

簠簋备列，粢盛隆丰。笾豆蠲洁，三牲肥充。
笙镛和鸣，佾舞称容。神其来格，享此献奉。[1]

生民之初，心智懵懵。彝伦不明[2]，长夜无穷。
尧舜禹汤，文武周公，庠序[3]养贤，开辟鸿蒙。

春秋季世，纪纲失统。忧道不行，木铎[4]警众。
杏坛设教，儒学大弘。倬彼云汉，为章苍穹。

为政以德，北辰是拱。仁孝为本，父子融融。

忠信相交，上下股肱[5]。日升月恒[6]，泮水辟雍[7]。

明德新民，君子之风。性情和达，乃为中庸。
诗礼传家，开我华风。立我烝[8]民，莫非尔功。

立己达人，四海弟兄。修齐治平，天下为公[9]。
文德既修，远方来朋。寅[10]协万邦，和而不同。

弥高弥坚，圣自天纵。照临千秋，为祷为颂。

2013年9月28日，时任山东省委常委、常务副省长孙伟恭读祭文。 （图片由济宁日报社刘项清拍摄）

On September 28th, 2013, Sun Wei, Member of the Standing Committee of the CPC Shandong Provincial Committee and Executive Vice Governor of Shandong Province at that time, solemnly recited the commemoration text.

神州复兴，百年之梦。法古开新，国祚久永。
伏惟尚飨！

◎ 注释

1. 簠簋备列，粢盛隆丰。笾豆蠲洁，三牲肥充。笙镛和鸣，佾舞称容。神其来格，享此献奉：簠是指古代祭祀时盛稻粱的器具；簋指的是古代盛食物的器具，圆口，双耳；粢盛指的是古代盛在祭器内以供祭祀的谷物；笾是指古代祭祀和宴会时盛果品等的竹器；蠲洁即指清洁。蠲，古同"涓"；镛指大钟，古代的一种乐器。

2. 彝伦不明：彝伦指常理，伦常。彝，常理。

3. 庠序：泛指学校。殷代叫庠，周代叫序。

4. 木铎：以木为舌的大铃，铜质。古代宣布政教法令时，巡行振鸣以引起众人注意。以喻宣扬教化的人。《论语·八佾》："天下之无道也久矣，天将以夫子为木铎。"

5. 股肱：大腿和胳膊。均为躯体的重要部分。引申为辅佐君主的大臣，又比喻左右辅助得力的人。

6. 日升月恒：旭日冉冉上升，月亮渐渐盈满。比喻事物兴盛发展。

7. 泮水辟雍：泮水，古代学宫前的水池，形状如半月；辟雍，辟，通"璧"。本为西周天子所设大学，校址圆形，围以水池，前门外有便桥。东汉以后，历代皆有辟雍，除北宋末年为太学之预备学校外，均为行乡饮、大射或祭祀之礼的地方。

8. 烝：众多。

9. 天下为公：原指君位不为一家私有，后为一种美好的社会政治理想。《礼记·礼运》："大道之行也，天下为公。"

10. 寅：敬。

◎ 译文

夏历癸巳年辛酉月丁酉日，是至圣先师孔子诞辰 2564 年，山东省人民政府奉以释奠大典、鲜花雅乐，庆祝孔子诞辰。向您祈求祷告：

伟大的孔夫子，像泰山那样高耸。他的道德崇高而盛大，天下人士普遍将他推重、尊崇。众多的人士严整恭敬，夫子庙堂乐声和谐。今天我们按照常礼举行祭祀，用来表示景仰与尊敬。簠与簋等祭祀礼器完备陈列，祭器内盛装供祭祀的谷物。笾与豆干净清洁，牛、羊、豕三牲齐备。笙与镛等乐器应和鸣响，祭祀乐舞齐备完整。希望孔子的神灵来到，享受这丰盛隆重的献奉。

人类产生之初，人们的心智懵懵懂懂还没有开化。人与人之间的相处之道尚未分明，简直就像长夜一样没有尽穷。尧、舜、禹、汤以及文王、武王、周公，开设学校教育百姓培养贤能，从而导引人们走出迷惘，创立了礼乐文明。春秋末年，天下的纲纪失去了统绪。孔子担心社会无道，于是宣扬教化来告诫和警醒世人。他设教收徒，开办私学，于是创立儒学，使道术得到大力弘扬。他的思想高入云霄，他的影响光耀九天。凭着自身的道德修养管理国家，就会像北极星被众星环绕那样。以仁爱孝悌为立身的根本，能使家庭和睦，其乐融融。按照忠诚信实的态度处理人际关系，就能上下倾力尽心。事业兴旺，教化流行，就像太阳升起，就像月亮初上。发扬好的德行，提升民众素养，君子般的道德风尚大行于世。人们性情和顺，为人处事就能中正不倚。以儒家经典和道德规范世代相传，由此开创了我中华民族的美好风尚。我中华民族生生不息，代代传承，难道不是孔子的功德。人修行自身，从而推己及人，四海之内都如同兄弟一般。人们修身、齐家、治国、平天下，以天下为天下人的天下。做好了礼乐教化，远处的朋友就能得到团结，从而与世界各国友好相处，处理好各种关系。孔子的思想越仰望越高大，越钻研越深刻，孔子才智超众，简直就是上天所赋予。希望孔子思想光耀千秋，我们祈祷，我们称颂。中华民族的复兴，是我们百年以来的梦想。继承传统文化服务于今天的事业，使之焕发出新的活力，必将国家富强，江山永固。

伏请您享用供品！

祭孔大典现场 　　　　　（图片由济宁日报社提供）

The scene of Confucius Commemoration Ceremony.

Text of the Guisi Year (2013) Confucius Commemoration Ceremony

Written by: Peng Lin

Now is the Year of the Water Snake on the traditional Chinese Lunar Calendar. Now is the Month of the Metal Rooster. On this day, the Day of the Fire Rooster, two thousand five hundred and sixty-four years have passed since the birth of our departed Master Confucius. On this day, the Shandong Provincial People's Government hereby presents a grand memorial ceremony with flowers and elegant music.

Using the words of the Great Sage to praise him:

The Holy Master is as great as the towering mountains. He gains virtue and respect throughout the whole land and from all the people.

Solemnly, many scholars gather together and fill the hall of the temple. In honor of him, ritual and sacrifice are performed one after another.

Abundant row upon row of offerings have been prepared. The sacrificial utensils are placed each in their proper place. The fatted calf, the suckling pig, and the young sheep have been prepared.

The reedpipe and giant bell sing out in harmony. A procession of dancers march forward in step. The spirits arrive to receive the sacrificial offerings.

When human beings first appeared on earth, people's hearts and minds had not been fully developed. Common sense is not common. The journey towards wisdom is one that never ends.

The four Wise Emperors (Tang Yao, Yu Shun, Xia Yu, and Shang Tang) created the laws that the Duke of Zhou further codified. Just as Pangu created order out of chaos, Confucius created an academy to nurture the virtuous.

During the Spring and Autumn era, discipline fell by the wayside. As the tolling bell warns, morality is more important than money.

Since the establishment of the Apricot Altar, from which he taught, Confucianism has began to spread throughout the land. The distant Milky Way spills across the vast arch of the sky.

A ruler who governs with virtue and morality is like the north star dwelling in his place and surrounded by other stars in an orderly manner. With benevolence and filial piety as the foundation, relationships between fathers and sons are harmonious.

Loyalty and trust, superior and inferior, up and down, they all intersect and interact. By the rising sun and the constant moon, may the wisdom pouring out from the Academy flood the halls of government.

Bright virtue is blinded and suppressed by material interests. Virtue can be revealed with proper education, and by constantly striving to improve, a gentleman can contribute his virtue to society. A harmonious temperament is called moderation.

Establishing the Chinese style, the Confucian classics and their moral norms have been passed down from generation to generation. Establish oneself as a servant of the people, and refrain from belittling one's own accomplishments.

If you want to establish yourself, you must also help others to establish themselves; if you want to achieve enlightenment, you must also help others achieve it together. In this way, the whole world can become brothers. For all things in the world to serve the common good, it is necessary to cultivate the self, manage well both family and country, and appease the common people's aspirations.

Cultivate both literature and virtue for friends from near and far. Unity and harmony among all parties do not require uniformity.

Stronger, firmer, greater, these are the virtues that come from Heaven. Shining throughout the ages, praised in prayer and song.

The revival of China is a century-old dream. Ancient philosophy creates new ideas that will lead the country to flourish for ever and ever.

Of this, I respectfully beseech you!

彭林简介

彭　林: 1949年生，江苏无锡人，清华大学人文学院历史系教授、博士生导师。兼任国际儒学联合会理事，中国社会科学院古代文明研究中心客座研究员，清华大学古典文献研究中心客座研究员，中国人民大学国学院学术委员会委员、客座教授，北京师范大学宗教与人文高等研究中心学术研究部主任，《中国经学》主编等。

研究领域：中国古代学术思想史、历史文献学和礼乐文化。

主要著作：《周礼主体思想与成书年代研究》《文物精品与文化中国》《中国古代礼仪文明》《中国礼学在古代朝鲜的播迁》《礼乐中华》等。整理古籍《周礼注疏》《仪礼注疏》。

Introduction to Peng Lin

Peng Lin, born in 1949 in Wuxi, Jiangsu Province, is a professor and doctoral supervisor in the Department of History at the School of Humanities, Tsinghua University. He also serves as a director of the International Confucian Association, a visiting researcher at the Ancient Civilization Research Center of the Chinese Academy of Social Sciences, and a visiting researcher at the Classical Literature Research Center of Tsinghua University. Additionally, he is a member of the Academic Committee and a visiting professor at the Academy of Confucian Studies, Renmin University of China, and the chief editor of "Chinese Classics."

His research primarily focuses on the history of ancient Chinese academic thought, historical philology, and ritual and music culture.

His major works include "Research on the Main Ideas and Compilation Date of Zhou Li," "Fine Cultural Relics and Cultural China," "Ancient Chinese Ritual Civilization," "The Spread of Chinese Ritual Studies in Ancient Korea," and "Chinese Rites and Music." He has also compiled ancient texts such as "Annotations and Explanations of Zhou Li" and "Annotations and Explanations of Yi Li."

2014 甲午年
弘扬优秀传统文化
共建文明首善之区

2014, the Year of Jiawu.
Promoting excellent traditional culture, co-building the
epitome of civilization.

纪念孔子诞辰 2565 年

Commemorating the 2565th Anniversary of Confucius's Birth

甲午（2014）年祭孔大典祭文

张立文　撰

惟夏历甲午之岁，恭逢先师孔子诞辰 2565 年，谨以香花酒果，佾舞雅乐，敬奠于夫子暨诸圣哲之灵。其辞曰：

天地何来？人类何生？和实生物，同则不继。[1]
阴阳纲缊[2]，五行相杂。万物化醇，实惟纲纪。

汤武革命，应天顺人。惟德是辅，敬德保民。[3]
水能载覆，民贵君轻。无信不立，去食去兵。[4]

巍巍孔子，圣道昭明。复兴礼乐，挽澜扶倾。
己达达人，博施于民。惟圣之德，万世永馨。

天道刚健，地道柔顺。人道仁义，天下文明。
天文察变，人文化成。[5] 诚意正心，修齐治平。[6]

知行合一，推己及人。仁爱民本，诚信正义。[7]
洪惟中华，绍宏文化。道德精髓，至善知止。

势利纷华，不染尤洁。君子九德，进退守正。[8]
礼义为纪，各正性命。经国序民，坤宁乾清。

多重世界，差分融突。和而不同，协和万邦。
和平发展，合作共赢。命运同体，寰宇辉煌。

天人和美，身心和乐。家和则兴，国和则强。

2014 年 9 月 28 日，时任山东省委副书记、省长郭树清恭读祭文。 （图片由济宁日报社刘项清拍摄）

On September 28th, 2014, Guo Shuqing, Deputy Secretary of the CPC Shandong Provincial Committee and Governor of Shandong Province at that time, solemnly recited the commemoration text.

革故鼎新，自强不息。和合世界，幸福永享。
伏惟尚飨！

◎ 注释

1. 和实生物，同则不继：实现和谐则万物生长繁衍，如果完全一致，则无法发展延续。《国语·郑语》："夫和实生物，同则不继。以他平他谓之和，故能丰长而物生之。若以同裨同，尽乃弃矣。"

2. 阴阳绸缊：阴阳二气在天地间缭绕交缠互相作用。《易·系辞下》："天地氤氲，万物化醇；男女构精，万物化生。"

3. 汤武革命，应天顺人。惟德是辅，敬德保民：《易·革》："汤武革命，顺乎天而应乎人。"《书·蔡仲之命》："皇天无亲，惟德是辅。"周公制礼作乐，有一个基本的指导思想，即"敬德保民"。"敬德"，是因为"皇天无亲，惟德是辅"，有德才会得到上天的保佑。"保民"，是因为"民之所欲，天必从之"，"保民"实际上就是保社稷、保国家。

4. 水能载覆，民贵君轻。无信不立，去食去兵：《荀子·哀公》："孔子曰：'丘闻之：君者，舟也；庶人者，水也；水则载舟，水则覆舟。'"《孟子·尽心下》："民为贵，社稷次之，君为轻。"《论语》："子贡问政。子曰：'足食，足兵，民信之矣。'子贡曰：'必不得已而去，于斯三者何先？'曰：'去兵。'子贡曰：'必不得已而去，于期二者何先？'曰："去食。自古皆有死，民无信不立。'"

5. 天文察变，人文化成：《易·象》："刚柔交错，天文也；文明以止，人文也。观乎天文，以察时变；观乎人文，以化成天下。"意思是治国者要察看天气变化发展农业生产，把握好人伦秩序就可以让人民文明有序。

6. 修齐治平：《礼记·大学》："古之欲明明德于天下者，先治其国；欲治其国者，先齐其家；欲齐其家者，先修其身；欲修其身者，先正其心；欲正其心者，先诚其意；欲诚其意者，先致其知，致知在格物。"

7. 仁爱民本，诚信正义：习近平总书记在 2014 年 2 月主持中央政治局集体学习时强调："要挖掘、阐发中华优秀传统文化讲仁爱、重民本、守诚信、崇正义、尚和合、求大同的时代价值。"

8. 势利纷华，不染尤洁。君子九德，进退守正：明·洪应明《菜根谭》："势利纷华，不近者为洁；近之而不染者为尤洁。"《书·皋陶谟》："皋陶曰：都，亦行有九德，亦言其人有德，乃言曰载采采。禹曰：何？皋陶曰：宽而栗、柔而立、愿而恭、乱而敬、扰而毅、直而温、简而廉、刚而塞、强而义、彰厥有常，吉哉！"《史记·礼书》："循法守正者见侮于世，奢溢僭差者谓之显荣。"《旧唐书》："上为太子时，知其进退守正，及是用为宰相，甚礼信之。"这两句话的意思是显赫的权势、优厚的利益以及令人眼花缭乱的虚名，不去接近是志向高洁，然而，接近了却不受污染则更为品质高尚。正人君子具有九大美好的品行，面对利害得失都会坚守正道。

◎ 译文

夏历甲午年（2014 年），是至圣先师孔子诞辰 2565 年，恭敬地奉上香花酒果、佾舞雅乐告慰夫子及诸先哲先贤。祭文是：

天地从何而来？人类从何而生？实现和谐则万物生长繁衍，如果完全一致，则无法发展延续。阴阳二气相互反应，金木水火土交相混合，生成万物精灵，我们要恭敬小心地顺从这一法则。商汤和周武王以武力推翻前朝，乃是顺应天命，合乎人心。只有品德好才会得到上天的保佑，重视道德才会安保社稷。水能载船，也能把船打翻，所以人民要比统治者重要。国家得不到人民的信任就会垮掉，宁可放弃粮食和军备也不要放弃人民的信任。

伟大的孔子啊，他的学说大放光明。复兴周公的礼乐，努力改变礼崩乐坏的现实。自己得到了，然后也帮助别人得到，给人民带来很多好处。孔子的道德品行，是千秋万代永恒的精神支柱。天道刚健，地道柔顺，人道仁义，这三样东西都具备了，天下就文明有序了。治国者要察看天气变化发展农业生产，把握好人伦秩序就可以让人民文明有序。意念诚实、保持心灵的安静，就可以不断提高自己的品德修养，让自己的家庭和睦，处理好政务，让天下太平。知行合一、推己及人、仁爱民本、诚信正义，是当今我们培育和弘扬的时代价值。博大的传统文化，要继承和弘扬。道德的精髓在于使人达到最完善的境界。显赫的权势、优厚的利益以及令人眼花缭乱的虚名，不去接近是志向高洁，然而，接近了却不受污染则更为品质高尚。正人君子具有九大美好的品行，面对利害得失都会坚守正道。以礼作为道德的行为标准，分别遵从固有的自然规律、社会规律。礼可以治理好国家、安抚好百姓，从而达到天下太平。

当今世界多元化，不同的文明相互融合、冲突。只有坚持不同文明的和谐共处，才可以让国际社会和谐发展。各国都要和平发展，相互合作追求互利共赢。共同遵守这一发展思路，就会建设更加辉煌美好的世界。自然与人类和谐，就会美好；人的生理与心理和谐，就会快乐。家庭和谐就会兴旺，国家和谐就会富强。与大自然保持和谐，就会得到"天乐"；与百姓融洽相处，就会得到"人乐"。这样，世界就会和谐，人民永享幸福安康。

伏请您享用供品！

祭孔大典现场 　　（图片由济宁日报社提供）

The scene of Confucius Commemoration Ceremony.

Text of the Jiawu Year (2014) Confucius Commemoration Ceremony

Written by: Zhang Liwen

Now is the Year of the Wood Horse on the traditional Chinese Lunar Calendar. It is also the 2,565th anniversary of the birth of our departed Master Confucius. With fragrant flowers, wine, and fruits, we dance to elegant music and pay homage to the Master and to the spirits of all sages. Using the words of the Great Sage to praise him:

Where do the Earth and Heaven come from? From where do people come from? Life is born from disharmony.

Yin and yang, dark and light, and the five elements create the universe by generating and inhibiting each other. All things move and change, but laws of nature are fixed.

As people with high moral character respect virtue and help and protect others, it was destined that the Xia Dynasty would be overthrown by the Shang Dynasty.

The water that supports a ship can also capsize it; the common man is more important than the nobles. Without faith, there is no nation, no supplies, no military.

Magnificent Confucius, teacher of the holy way. Reviving the proper observance of ritual and music, reversing a tide of neglect and dissolution.

If you decide to be tolerant of others, others will be tolerant of you. This brings benefits to everyone. The innate virtues of the holy sages will lead to happiness throughout the ages.

The way of Heaven is firm, and the way of Earth is pliable. Humanity, benevolence, and righteousness make the world civilized.

As the skies above gradually change, so too does humanity evolve. A sincere and upright person cultivates the self, manages well his or her family and country, and helps to appease the common people's aspirations in the world.

Unite knowledge with action, and promote yourself and others. Benevolence to the people, integrity, and justice.

China inherits our predecessors' cultural legacy of broad-mindedness, love of education, and benevolence. The essence of morality is the ultimate knowledge.

To be close to power and wealth and remain uncorrupted is greater than to be pure without temptation. The nine virtues of a gentleman require both giving and taking. He is to be broad-minded and yet apprehensive, to be soft and yet steadfast, to be sincere and yet respectful, to reform and yet be cautious, to be troublesome and yet perseverant, direct yet gentle, simple yet incorruptible, hard yet restrained, and strong yet righteous.

Etiquette and righteousness are the criteria by which people rectify their nature and destiny. The heavens are clear, the air is clean, the nation is peaceful, and the people are safe.

Differing points of view are merging and melding. Harmony among all parties does not require uniformity.

Peaceful development and win-win cooperation. Shared destiny in a brilliant world.

Harmony between man and nature is beautiful; harmony in body and mind is joyous. When harmony is found at the household level, all is prosperous. When the country is harmonious, the people experience great benefits.

Reform the old, create the new, and constantly strive for self-improvement. May the world find harmony and enjoy eternal happiness.

I respectfully beseech you!

张立文简介

张立文：1935 年生，浙江温州人，著名哲学家、哲学史家。中国人民大学哲学院一级教授、哲学院博士生导师，中国人民大学孔子研究院院长、学术委员会主席，中国传统文化研究中心主任；曾任中国人民大学和合文化研究所所长。兼任中国周易研究会副会长、国际儒学联合会顾问、国际易学联合会理事、国际退溪学会理事、日本东京大学客座研究员、中国炎黄文化研究会理事、中国文化书院导师等。

研究领域：中国哲学、中国文化的教学研究。

主要著作：出版《中国哲学逻辑结构论》《传统学引论》《新人学导论》《和合学——21 世纪文化战略的构想》《朱熹思想研究》等。主编、合著《中国学术通史》（六卷本）、《中外儒学比较研究》、《传统文化与现代文化丛书》、《东亚哲学与21 世纪丛书》等 40 多本。在国内外报刊发表学术论文 500 多篇。

Introduction to Zhang Liwen

Zhang Liwen, born in 1935 in Wenzhou, Zhejiang Province, is a renowned philosopher and historian of philosophy. He is a first-level professor and doctoral supervisor at the School of Philosophy, Renmin University of China, and serves as the Dean and Chairman of the Academic Committee of the Confucius Institute at Renmin University of China, as well as the Director of the Center for Traditional Chinese Culture. He previously held positions as the director of the Renmin University of China and Hehe Cultural Research Institute. Additionally, he holds various other positions such as Vice President of the Chinese Yi Studies Association, Consultant of the International Confucian Association, Director of the International Yi Studies Association, Director of the International Toegye Studies Association, Visiting Researcher at the University of Tokyo, and Mentor at the Chinese Culture Academy.

His research primarily focuses on the teaching and research of Chinese philosophy and culture.

His major works include "Logic Structure Theory of Chinese Philosophy," "Introduction to Traditional Studies," "Introduction to New Confucianism," "Harmony Studies: Vision for Cultural Strategy in the 21st Century," and "Study on the Thought of Zhu Xi." He has also edited or co-authored over 40 books, including "General History of Chinese Studies" (six volumes), "Comparative Studies of Chinese and Foreign Confucianism," "Series on Traditional Culture and Modern Culture," and

"Series on East Asian Philosophy and the 21st Century." He has published over 500 academic papers in domestic and international journals. His works have received numerous awards, including the Excellent Achievement Award from Beijing Municipality, the Ministry of Education, and the National Social Science Fund, as well as the International Toegye Academic Award. He has been included in various domestic and international directories of distinguished individuals, including those from Cambridge, the United States, and India.

2015 乙未年

弘扬优秀传统文化
建设文明首善之区

2015, the Year of Yiwei.
Promoting excellent traditional culture, co-building the
epitome of civilization.

纪念孔子诞辰2566年

Commemorating the 2566th Anniversary of Confucius's Birth

乙未（2015）年祭孔大典祭文

钱　逊　撰

维此乙未仲秋，公历 2015 年 9 月 28 日，乃至圣先师孔子二千五百六十六年诞辰，吾等华夏胞民，谨具鲜卉果蔬，佾舞雅乐，肃祭圣师，恭献此文。

圣师孔子，生于无道之世，力倡雅颂之声[1]。承尧舜禹汤文武之余绪，集礼乐射御书数[2]之大成，设帐授徒，创立儒宗，开百代之圣教，化万民于春风。

圣师之教，垂范至今。以人为本，不语乱神[3]；以德为政[4]，立己立人。兴学杏坛，有教无类[5]；文行忠信[6]，约礼博文[7]。三千弟子，传道四海；泽被天下，十步芳邻。乐群贵和[8]，行己有耻[9]；修齐治平[10]，遍惠人伦。洵为万世之师表，五洲之圣哲，凝华夏之魂魄，涌文明之朝暾[11]。

近世以降，西风东凌。圣师之言犹在，而或成腐儒之虚饰，或遭伪士之凶讦。然礼失诸庙堂，犹可求诸四野，况志士仁人迭起，力挽神州陆沉。圣贤之道，潜而复苏，忠恕之义，普世皆钦。今日华夏，病夫之名已去，而全盛之日未临，诚宜秉传圣训，固本培根，崇德以筑中国梦，旧命而维天下新。乐宾朋来自四海，绘丹青馈于子孙。幸我九州通力，朝野一心，华夏之洪舟，正扬帆破浪而进。谨以此告，先师圣灵。伏惟尚飨，日升月恒！

2015年9月28日，时任山东省委副书记龚正恭读祭文。 （图片由济宁日报社刘项清拍摄）

On September 28th, 2015, Gong Zheng, Deputy Secretary of the CPC Shandong Provincial Committee at that time, solemnly recited the commemoration text.

◎ 注释

1. 雅颂之声：亦作"雅讼"。《诗经》内容和乐曲分类的名称。有诗句"三光日月星，四诗风雅颂"，"诗"指的"诗经"，它由《风》《雅》《颂》组成；"雅"又分"大雅""小雅"，合起来是四部分。雅乐为朝廷的乐曲，颂为宗庙祭祀的乐曲。也指盛世之乐、庙堂之乐。

2. 礼乐射御书数：为春秋战国时期读书人必须学习的六种技艺，分别为礼法、乐舞、射箭、驾车、书法和算术。其中射箭、驾车（御战车）为军事技能。

3. 不语乱神："子不语怪力乱神"出自《论语·述而》，孔子不谈论怪异、勇力、叛乱和鬼神。

4. 以德为政：为政以德是儒家主张的治国基本原则，即指用道德教化来治理人民。《论语·为政》："子曰：'为政以德，譬如北辰，居其所而众星共之。'""'道之以政，齐之以刑，民免而无耻。道之以德，齐之以礼，有耻且格。'"

5. 有教无类：《论语·卫灵公》："子曰：'有教无类。'"类：种类，指教育不分高低贵贱，对各类人都一视同仁。

6. 文行忠信：《论语·述而》："子以四教：文，行，忠，信。"即指孔子以四项内容来教导学生：文化知识、履行所学之道的行动、忠诚、守信。

7. 约礼博文：《论语·雍也》："君子博学于文，约之以礼，亦可以弗畔矣夫！"意思是广求学问，恪守礼法。

8. 乐群贵和："仁爱"思想是儒家思想中的核心概念之一，主张尊重人、理解人、关心人、帮助人、爱护人、同情人，讲求谦敬礼让，倡导团结友爱，强调社会和谐，追求与自然和谐、人际和谐、身心和谐。

9. 行己有耻：《论语·子路》："行己有耻，使于四方，不辱君命，可谓士矣。"意指一个人行事，凡自己认为可耻的就不去做。

10. 修齐治平：《礼记·大学》："古之欲明明德于天下者，先治其国；欲治其国者，先齐其家；欲齐其家者，先修其身。"指提高自身修为，管理好家庭，治理好国家，安抚天下百姓苍生的抱负。

11. 曦：指初升的太阳。

◎ 译文

乙未年仲秋时节，公历 2015 年 9 月 28 日，时值至圣先师孔子 2566 年诞辰。华夏同胞们恭敬地备好鲜卉果蔬、佾舞雅乐，庄重地祭祀先师孔子，诚敬地献上这篇祭文。

圣师孔子，生于周朝衰落、礼崩乐坏的时期，试图恢复和重建礼乐精神。继承了尧、舜、禹、商汤、周文王、周武王的思想理念，集礼法、乐舞、射箭、驾车、书法和算术之大成于一身。设立讲座，传授生徒，创立儒家学派，开创了千秋万代的圣人之教，他的教化像春风化雨一般润物于无声，感化万民。

圣师孔子的教诲流传至今，在当今社会仍有深远影响。孔子主张以人为本，不谈论怪异、勇力、叛乱和鬼神；主张为政者要用道德教化来治理人民，修行自身并推己及人。在杏坛兴办私学，主张教育不分高低贵贱，一视同仁。以文、行、忠、信四项内容教导学生，广求学问、恪守礼法。门下弟子三千，将孔子教诲传遍五湖四海；孔子思想和德行惠及万民，主张乐群贵和的道德规范，构建和谐友爱的人际关系，不做令人耻辱的事情；主张修齐治平的思想，恩惠遍及百姓。孔子不愧为万世师表、五洲圣哲，凝聚着华夏精神，像朝阳一样照亮了整个中华文明的历史进程。

自近代以来，西方列强侵略中国，社会动荡不安。虽然孔子的教诲依然存在，然而有时遭遇"迷信""信古""反古""复古"的"腐儒"之流曲解，或被伪善之人恶意攻击。虽然孔子倡导的礼制思想被曲解攻击，但仍可以到民间去寻求和实践，更何况有志之士和仁人君子相继出现，致力于挽回神州陆沉的趋势。圣贤先哲的思想虽然暂时失去了它的光彩，但

祭孔大典现场　　　　　　　（图片由济宁日报社提供）

The scene of Confucius Commemoration Ceremony.

最终会重新复苏，忠恕仁义的思想，将会被全世界的人们所敬仰和推崇。当今的华夏，"东亚病夫"的污名已经消失，但尚未迎来全盛的时代。我们应该秉持圣人的教诲，巩固根本，培养人才，崇德向善，实现中华民族伟大复兴的中国梦。革故鼎新、去粗取精，不断适应新的形势和变化，为世界的繁荣和发展做出贡献。四海的宾朋纷至沓来，美好的生活献与子孙，中华人民万众一心，齐心协力，华夏的巨轮正扬帆起航，踏浪前行！谨以此告慰先师的圣灵。

伏请您享用供品，愿您的思想如同太阳和月亮的光辉恒久不灭！

Text of the Yiwei Year (2015) Confucius Commemoration Ceremony

Written by: Qian Xun

On the Chinese Lunar Calendar, it is the middle of autumn in the Year of the Wood Goat. On the Gregorian Calendar, it is September 28, 2015. Two thousand, five hundred and sixty-six years have passed since the birth of our departed Master Confucius. We, the sons and daughters of China, gather with fresh flowers, fruits, and vegetables to dance to elegant music and pay homage to the Holy Master.

Thus, do I speak the following:

Born in a world without virtue, the saintly teacher Confucius advocated for elegance and etiquette.

Inheriting the governing thoughts of the six Wise Emperors (Tang Yao, Yu Shun, Xia Yu, and Shang Tang, King Wen and Wu of zhou Dynasty), he collected rituals and music and promoted archery and the cataloging of great books.

From this, he taught his disciples, founded Confucianism, established the holy religion that lasted for hundreds of generations. His teachings were like spring breeze and rain moistering people's hearts silently.

The teachings of the Holy Master remain an example to this day.

People-oriented, put people first, and never talk nonsense; govern with virtue; to improve yourself means to improve others.

As the creator of the Apricot Altar and its lessons from which one can learn for all eternity, the Master taught literature, moral education, loyalty, and honesty, to abide by proper etiquette and seek knowledge widely.

His three thousand disciples publicized his words throughout the world, blessing and extending favor to all people under Heaven.

It is honorable to be happy at things that benefit the common good, but to act selfishly is shameful; to cultivate the self, manage well your family and country, and appease the common people's aspirations in the world will benefit human relations everywhere. Truly the teacher of all ages of mankind, the sage of the five continents, distills and spreads the essence of China's spiritual soul and motive force.

In modern times, China was invaded by Western powers. Despite suffering fierce criticism by hypocrites or becoming an affectation of corrupted thought, the words of the Holy Master remain pure.

Although Confucius's ritual thoughts might be misinterpreted at times, we can still seek help from all directions. No matter what, those who love and contribute to the motherland appear over and over to offer succor from enemies.

The way of the sages is to provide a path out of the darkness. Loyalty and forgiveness are universally admired.

The China of today has lost the title of "sick man." Although health has arrived, that does not yet mean flourishing prosperity. Thus, it is advisable to sincerely uphold the teachings of the Holy Scriptures to consolidate our roots, to advocate morality in the building of the Chinese dream, and to use old wisdom in the creation of a new world.

Offering ritual sacrifices, guests and friends from all over the world donate their strength. Working together with vim and vigor, the government and the public are united, and the great ark of our Chinese nation is slicing through the waves.

I would like to say this to you, oh spirit of our departed Master.

By the rising sun and the eternal moon, I respectfully beseech you!

钱逊简介

钱　逊：1933年生，江苏无锡人，国学大师钱穆之子。清华大学人文学院历史系、思想文化研究所教授。历任中华孔子学会副会长、国际儒学联合会副理事长，中国哲学史学会、中华炎黄文化研究会和中国孔子基金会理事等职。

2019年8月22日凌晨，钱逊逝世，享年86岁。

研究领域：先秦儒学、中国古代人生哲学。

主要著作：《论语浅解》《先秦儒学》《中国古代人生哲学》《推陈出新——传统文化在现代的发展》《中国传统道德》（全书副主编，《理论卷》主编）及论文若干篇。

Introduction to Qian Xun

Qian Xun, born in 1933 in Wuxi, Jiangsu Province, was the son of the renowned sinologist Qian Mu. He served as a professor at the Department of History and the Institute of Intellectual History at Tsinghua University. Throughout his career, he held various positions such as Vice President of the Chinese Confucius Association, Vice Chairman of the International Confucian Association, and Director of the Chinese Society for the History of Philosophy, the Chinese Yanhuang Culture Research Association, and the China Confucius Foundation.

On August 22, 2019, Qian Xun passed away at the age of 85.

His research primarily focused on Confucianism in the Pre-Qin period and ancient Chinese philosophy of life.

His major works include "An Introduction to the Analects of Confucius," "Confucianism in the Pre-Qin Period," "Ancient Chinese Philosophy of Life," and "Traditional Chinese Ethics" (as co-editor-in-chief and editor of the theoretical volume). He also authored "Innovation in Tradition: The Development of Traditional Culture in Modern Times" as well as several academic papers.

2016 丙申年

弘扬优秀传统文化
建设文明首善之区

2016, the Year of Bingshen.
Promoting excellent traditional culture, co-building the
epitome of civilization.

纪念孔子诞辰

2567

年

Commemorating the 2567th Anniversary of Confucius's Birth

丙申（2016）年祭孔大典祭文

颜炳罡　撰

维公元二〇一六年九月二十八，岁在丙申，序在仲秋，值天高气爽、花果飘香时节，山东各界人士、世界各地炎黄子孙、五洲宾朋等齐聚曲阜孔庙大成殿前，以至诚之心，崇敬之情，谨备蔬果，献以佾舞，敬祷于夫子及诸贤哲大儒神位。辞曰：

天地氤氲[1]，燮理阴阳，衮衮华胄，诞育东方。
荜路蓝缕[2]，野居草莽。三皇五帝，始创典章。
吊民伐罪[3]，商汤武王。降至春秋，渐失王纲。
礼坏乐崩[4]，五霸逞强。
大哉夫子，应时而降。宪章文武[5]，道承三皇。
杏坛设教，门开八方。三千弟子[6]，大道阐扬。
退修诗书，六艺始彰。韦编三绝[7]，行囊居床。
人文化成[8]，道始以昌。
以仁释礼，仁礼双彰。为仁由己[9]，无欲则刚。
孝悌忠恕，践仁之方。四勿四毋[10]，克己自强。
内省不疚，无愧俯仰[11]。中庸为德[12]，君子坦荡。

贫而好学，富而礼让 [13]。不怨不尤，知命守常。

仁为己任，弘毅担当。杀身成仁，以义为上。天何言哉？四时行焉，百物生长。[14]

道易天下，何计栖遑？天纵之圣，木铎 [15] 声响！

为政以德 [16]，举贤让良。正己正人，万民所望，

富而后教 [17]，礼乐兴邦。宽猛相济 [18]，治国有常。

博施济众 [19]，百姓安康。和而不同，德化万邦。

四海一家，大同在望。

大哉夫子，万世师表， 四海咸仰。

圣哉夫子，辉光日新，千秋传唱。

神哉夫子，明德赫赫，大道荡荡。

敬祷夫子，再现灵光，佑我华夏，保我家邦。

中国梦圆，华族永昌。以

复圣颜子

宗圣曾子

述圣子思子

亚圣孟子及诸大贤哲先儒

伏维尚飨！

2016年9月28日，时任山东省委常委、宣传部部长孙守刚恭读祭文。（图片由济宁日报社刘项清拍摄）

On September 28th, 2016, Sun Shougang, Member of the Standing Committee of the CPC Shandong Provincial Committee and Derector-general of Publicity Department at that time, solemnly recited the commemoration text.

◎ 注释

1. 天地氤氲：氤氲，烟云弥漫的样子。古代指阴阳二气互相作用的状态。《易·系辞下》："天地氤氲，万物化醇。"

2. 荜路蓝缕：筚路，柴车；蓝缕，破旧的衣服。意为驾着简陋的柴车，穿着破烂的衣服去开辟土地，形容创业的艰苦。《左传·宣公十二年》："筚路蓝缕，以启山林。"荜同筚。

3. 吊民伐罪：吊民，慰问百姓；伐罪，讨伐有罪的人。《孟子·滕文公下》："诛其君，吊其民，如时雨降，民大悦。"

4. 礼坏乐崩：礼坏，礼制崩溃；乐崩，乐教毁坏。形容社会秩序混乱，道德风尚败坏。《汉书·武帝纪》："盖闻导民以礼，风之以乐。今礼坏乐崩，朕甚闵焉。"

5. 宪章文武：宪章，效法；文武，指周文王、周武王。指遵循古代儒家的传统立场。《礼记·中庸》："仲尼祖述尧舜，宪章文武。"

6. 三千弟子：指孔子培养的三千多名孔门弟子。《史记·孔子世家》："孔子以诗书礼乐教，弟子盖三千焉。"

7. 韦编三绝：指孔子勤读《易》，致使编联竹简的皮绳多次脱断。《史记·孔子世家》："读《易》，韦编三绝。"

8. 人文化成：意为强调文治。《易·象》："观乎天文，以察时变，观乎人文，以化成天下。"

9. 为仁由己：意为实行仁德，完全在于自己，表示做好事全凭自己作出决定。《论语·颜渊》："子曰：'为仁由己，而由乎人哉？'"

10. 四勿四毋：四项禁止与四条劝阻。《论语·颜渊》："子曰：'非礼勿视，非礼勿听，非礼勿言，非礼勿动。'"《论语·子罕》："子绝四：毋意，毋必，毋固，毋我。"

11. 无愧俯仰：指为人正直、坦荡，对上对下都问心无愧。《孟子·尽心上》："仰不愧于天，俯不愧于人。"

12. 中庸为德：中庸，孔子学说的一种最高道德标准。中，折中，调和，无过之也无不及。庸，平常，普通。《论语·雍也》："子曰：'中庸之为德也，其至矣乎！民鲜久矣。'"

13. 富而礼让：富有且谦谦有礼。《论语·学而》："子曰：'可也，未若贫而乐，富而好礼者也。'"

14. 天何言哉？四时行焉，百物生长：言，说；哉，语气词；百物，泛指各种事物。意为天说什么了？四季照样运行，百物照样生长。《论语·阳货》："子曰：'天何言哉？四时行焉，百物生焉，天何言哉？'"

15. 木铎：古代一种以木为舌、金属为框的响器，用以警醒民众。《论语·八佾》："天下之无道也久矣，以夫子为木铎。"

16. 为政以德：用道德教化治理国家。《论语·为政》："子曰：'为政以德，譬如北辰，居其所而众星共之。'"

17. 富而后教：在生活富足的基础上进行教育和教化。《论语·子路》："子适卫，冉有仆。子曰：'庶矣哉！'冉有曰：'既庶矣，又何加焉？'曰：'富之。'曰：'既富矣，又何加焉？'曰：'教之。'"

18. 宽猛相济：指宽容和严厉相互补充，宽和严两种手段一起使用。《左传·昭公二十年》："政宽则民慢，慢则纠之以猛，猛则民残，残则施之以宽。宽以济猛，猛以济宽，政是以和。"

19. 博施济众：博，广泛；济，救济。意为给予群众以恩惠和接济。《论语·雍也》："如有博施于民而能济众，何如？"

◎ 译文

在公元二〇一六年九月二十八，丙申年仲秋，天高气爽、花果飘香的时节，山东各界人士、世界各地炎黄子孙、五洲宾朋等齐聚曲阜孔庙大成殿前，以至诚崇敬的心情，准备蔬果，供奉乐舞，恭敬地祭拜夫子和诸位圣人先哲。祭文是：

天地由阴阳二气交合而成，调和治理阴阳二气，华夏的后裔诞生孕育在这里。人们一直过着蒙昧原始的生活。直到三皇五帝，才开始创设典章制度，人们过上有礼仪的生活。经过商汤灭夏武王伐纣，建立了新的统一的王朝，人民生活更加安定。但到了春秋时期，周天子逐渐失去了对诸侯的控制。礼制破坏，社会纲纪紊乱，春秋五霸割据一方，社会陷入混乱。

伟大的孔子，在这个时候出现。效法周文王、周武王之制，继承弘扬三皇之道。在杏坛开设教场，不分贫富贵贱广收学生。培养三千多名学生，阐发弘扬中华大道。孔子勤奋读书、废寝忘食，退出朝堂，专心研究、整理诗书等古代文化，六艺之教开始得到彰显。以礼仪规范教化天下，中华大道开始得以昌盛。

以仁爱精神充实礼仪规范，仁爱精神与礼仪规范都得到彰显。做不做仁人君子，完全在于自己的意愿。一个人如果没有个人私欲，就会变得刚强正直。孝、悌、忠、恕，是践行仁德的方法。做到四勿四毋，自我克制，自强不息。自我反省没有内疚的地方，无愧于天地与他人。中庸是道德准则里的最高表现，君子应当心胸坦荡。贫穷的人爱好学习大道，富有的人谦谦有礼。不怨天不尤人，乐天知命，安分守常。以实现仁德为自己的任务，意志坚强有担当。为正义牺牲生命，义是最可贵的。天何尝说话了呢？四季照常运行，百物照样生长。

以仁道改变天下，为栖栖惶惶又有什么好忧惧的呢？既然是"天纵之圣""天之木铎"，哪有不发声之理！以道德原则治理国家，推荐贤能之士，对待自己和对待别人的原则一样，正是万民所希望的。衣食满足后开始接受教育，儒家的礼乐教化可以使国家兴旺。政治措施要宽和严互相补充，这样国家才能长治久安。广泛而普遍地给百姓以恩惠和救济苍生大众，百姓才能安康。和睦地相处，但不随意附和，以道德来融合不同地域的人。不同地域的人都成了一家，大同世界马上就可以实现。

伟大的孔子呀，是世代老师的表率，各地的人都很敬仰。圣人孔子呀，在道德、文学、艺术等方面日有长进，被人千秋万代地传颂。神圣的孔子呀，您有着高尚的道德，崇高的思想，值得我们学习。

祈祷孔子，再次显灵，保佑我们中华民族，保佑我们的国家。中国梦能够实现，中华民族永远昌盛。

再请

复圣颜子

宗圣曾子

述圣子思子

亚圣孟子及诸位大贤先哲一起，

我们伏在地上恭敬地请诸位先圣先贤享用供品！

祭孔大典现场　　　　　　（图片由济宁日报社提供）

The scene of Confucius Commemoration Ceremony.

Text of the Bingshen Year (2016) Confucius Commemoration Ceremony

Written by: Yan Binggang

On the Gregorian Calendar, today is September 28, 2016. On the Chinese Lunar Calendar, it is the middle of autumn in the Year of the Fire Monkey. It is the time when the weather is crisp, and the flowers and fruits are at their most fragrant. People from all over Shandong, people from all over the world, and the descendants of a time before time have gathered in front of the Dacheng Hall in Qufu's Confucius Temple. With sincerity and reverence, they have prepared offerings of fruits and flowers and offerings of music and dance as they offer prayers to the Master and the other Confucian sages.

I offer up these words:

The way of Heaven is vast and unfathomable. Competent ministers assist the government in state affairs.

The mighty descendants of the Chinese nation—knowing that simple and humble origins do not prevent one from ascending to greatness, paid out in blood, sweat, and tears to create something from nothing. The Three Sovereigns and Five Emperors were the founders of the law.

Giving succor to the weak and punishing the guilty, the Shang Dynasty overthrew the Xia. Down through the ages to the Spring and Autumn Period, the kings gradually lost their power and majesty.

Proper observance of ritual and music was neglected, and the Five Hegemons lorded their strength over the people.

The great Master came at the right time. Using methods inherited from the Three Sovereigns of antiquity, he formulated a civil and military system.

Preaching from the Apricot Altar, his word spread out in all directions. His three thousand disciples publicized his words throughout the world.

Withdrawing from politics, Confucius concentrated on studying and organizing ancient cultural classics such as poems and books and the Six Arts (Ritual, Music, Archery, Chariot-driving, Calligraphy, and Mathematics). Educating the world about etiquette and standards, the Chinese Way began to prosper.

As humanity evolves and matures, the road to prosperity is found. Giving new values and connotations to traditional rituals, benevolence and courtesy are both evident. Treat yourself with honor and benevolence, resist selfish desires, and you will find strength.

Filial piety, loyalty, and forgiveness are the principles of benevolence. Abiding by the principles of self-improvement taught by the ancestors, guard oneself and strive for self-improvement.

Introspection without guilt is worthy of admiration. Moderation is a virtue, and a gentleman is magnanimous.

Being poor but willing to learn and improve is a way of life; being rich but polite is a value choice. Don't complain or be angry; know your destiny and keep to your own life.

It is our duty to be benevolent; taking responsibility shows strength of mind and character. It is just and right to sacrifice one's life on the altar of benevolence. Have the heavens said anything? To everything, there is a season for growing and prospering.

The world under Heaven is constantly changing, so why be restless and uncertain? Confucius, the sage of Heaven, sounded the clarion call for morality!

He promoted virtue, conducting government with morality, righteous behavior for oneself as an example to others, and hope for all people.

He understood that prosperity for the people was the prerequisite to further educating them and knew that proper actions in terms of ritual and etiquette would benefit all. Tolerance and strictness complement each other and result in an ordered nation,

Provide assistance to the masses, and everyone will be hale and healthy.

Virtuous coexistence between all parties does not require uniformity.

The whole world is one family, and achieving Great Harmony is within our sights.

Oh, Great Master, a teacher for all generations who is admired by the whole world.

Oh, Holy Master, your glory is renewed day by day, and you will be sung of for thousands of years.

Great and holy Master, your bright virtue is remarkable; your integrity is unswerving.

Great Master, your aura illuminates us: Bless China, protect my home and family.

The Chinese dream will come true; the Chinese people will find perpetual prosperity. Thanks to the Holy One Yan Hui, the Great One Zengzi, the Awesome One Zisi, the Amazing One Mencius, and all the other great sages and Confucian scholars, I give thanks again and again!

颜炳罡简介

颜炳罡：1960 年生，山东临沂人，现为山东大学哲学与社会发展学院教授、博士生导师，山东大学儒学高等研究院副院长，国际儒学联合会理事、国际儒学联合会学术委员会委员、中国哲学史学会理事、山东周易研究会副会长、山东孔子学会常务理事兼副秘书长、山东省中华诗文教育学会顾问、《孔子研究》编委、韩国成均馆大学《儒教文化研究》编委等。

研究领域：中国哲学，特别是儒家哲学的教学与研究。

主要著作：出版《整合与重铸——当代大儒牟宗三先生思想研究》《当代新儒学引论》《墨学与新文化建设》《慧命相续——熊十力》等；在《孔子研究》《文史哲》《哲学研究》《法言》《鹅湖》等海内外学术刊物上发表论文 60 多篇。

Introduction to Yan Binggang

Yan Binggang, born in 1960 in Linyi, Shandong Province, is currently a professor and doctoral supervisor at the School of Philosophy and Social Development at Shandong University. He also serves as the Vice Dean of the Shandong University Institute of Confucian Studies. Additionally, he holds positions such as Director of the International Confucian Association, Member of the Academic Committee of the International Confucian Association, Director of the Chinese Society for the History of Philosophy, Vice President of the Shandong Yi Jing Research Association, Executive Director and Deputy Secretary-General of the Shandong Confucius Society, Advisor to the Shandong Chinese Poetry and Literature Education Society, Editorial Board Member of "Confucius Studies," and Editorial Board Member of "Confucian Culture Research" at South Korea's Sungkyunkwan University.

His research primarily focuses on Chinese philosophy, especially Confucian philosophy, with an emphasis on teaching and research.

His major works include "Integration and Recasting: A Study of the Thought of the Contemporary Great Confucian Mou Zongsan," "An Introduction to Contemporary Neo-Confucianism," "Mohism and the Construction of New Culture," and "Continuation of Wisdom and Life: Xiong Shili." He has published over 60 papers in academic journals both domestically and internationally, including "Confucius Studies," "Journal of Literature, History, and Philosophy," "Philosophical Research," "Law and Speech," and "Goose Lake."

2017 丁酉年
用儒家文化讲好中国故事

2017, the Year of Dingyou.
Telling China's stories with Confucian culture.

纪念孔子诞辰 2568 年

Commemorating the 2568th Anniversary of Confucius's Birth

丁酉（2017）年祭孔大典祭文

潘鲁生　召集

维公元 2017 年 9 月 28 日，岁在丁酉，时在金秋。值此夫子诞辰之日，各界人士以虔诚之心、崇仰之情，谨以释奠大典，祗告于先师之圣灵。

其文曰：

煌煌中华，郁郁文明，尧舜禹汤，文武周公。
圣哉夫子，如岳之耸，弘道明德，地纬天经。
祖述宪章，删述六经，杏坛设教，儒学肇兴。
仁义礼智，絜矩[1]中正，推己及人，一以贯通。

西狩获麟，纲纪失统，怨祸构连，饥馑频仍。
千秋荣辱，百代废兴，斗转参横，沐雨栉风。
崇文兴学，开辟鸿蒙，人知所止，福善盈盈[2]。
立我烝民[3]，以理以风，惟此圣道，曷可弗宗[4]？

嗟我夫子，既圣且明，述而识文，作而知情。
垂仪立极[5]，山海麟凤，生民未有，卓乎独盛。

弟子拱辰，后学述宗，章句汉唐，义理宋明。
和合阴阳，物阜民丰，万世师表，天地同功。

荡荡德风[6]，熠熠儒行[7]，仁爱诚信，民族魂灵。
讲信修睦[8]，家国以宁，近悦远来[9]，四方和同。
规矩方圆，人和政通，修齐治平[10]，神州复兴。
敬祷夫子，克鉴斯诚！佑我中华，以昌以隆！

伏惟尚飨！

2017 年 9 月 28 日，时任山东省委副书记、省长
龚正恭读祭文。　　（图片由济宁日报社刘项清拍摄）

On September 28th, 2017, Gong Zheng, Deputy Secretary of the
CPC Shandong Provincial Committee and Governor of Shandong
Province at that time, solemnly recited the commemoration text.

◎ 注释

1. 絜矩：絜，度量；矩，画方形的用具，引申为法度。儒家以絜矩来象征道德上的规范。《礼记·大学》："所谓平天下在治其国者，上老老而民兴孝，上长长而民兴弟，上恤孤而民不倍，是以君子有絜矩之道也。"

2. 福善盈盈：福善，福德善行。汉·焦赣《易林·屯之既济》："福善并作，乐以高明。"《诗·小雅·南有嘉鱼之什》："福祉满盈，年岁大丰。"

3. 立我烝民：使百姓安定。《诗·周颂》："思文后稷，克配彼天。立我烝民，莫匪尔极。"

4. 曷可弗宗：怎么能够不效法。《御制重修孔子庙碑》："曰惟圣道，曷敢弗宗。"

5. 立极：树立最高准则。唐·杜甫《有事于南郊赋》："所以报本反始，所以庆长立极。"

6. 德风：《论语·颜渊》："君子之德风，小人之德草。草上之风，必偃。"邢昺疏："在上君子，为政之德若风；在下小人，从化之德如草。"后因称君子为政之德为德风。唐·宋璟《奉和圣制送张说巡边》："德风边草偃，胜气朔云平。"

7. 儒行：儒家的道德规范或行为准则，也指合乎儒教的言行。《礼记·儒行》："哀公曰：'敢问儒行？'"南朝·梁·刘峻《辩命论》："瓛则关西孔子，通涉六经，循循善诱，服膺儒行。"唐·刘长卿 《淮上送梁二恩命追赴上都》："贾生年最少，儒行汉庭闻。"

8. 讲信修睦：讲究信用，睦邻修好。《礼记·礼运》："选贤与能，讲信修睦。"

9. 近悦远来：近居的人悦服，远处的人慕化而来。形容政治清明，远近归附。《论语·子路》："叶公问政，子曰：'近者说，远者来。'"

10. 修齐治平：修身、齐家、治国、平天下的省称。《礼记·大学》："古之欲明明德于天下者，先治其国；欲治其国者，先齐其家；欲齐其家者，先修其身。"

◎ 译文

在公元 2017 年 9 月 28 日，丁酉年的金秋时节，孔子诞辰日，各界人士怀着虔诚崇仰的心情，恭敬地用释奠的礼节祭拜先师孔子。祭文是：

辉煌灿烂的中华，文化繁盛，先后出现了唐尧、虞舜、夏禹、商汤、周文王、周武王、周公。孔子圣明啊，像五岳那样崇高，弘扬正道，彰显美德，阐明了天地之间的无可非议的道理。遵循效法之前圣人之道，修订了《诗》《书》《礼》《乐》《易》《春秋》经典。孔子在杏坛办学，儒学得以兴起。提倡做人要仁、义、礼、智等道德规范纯正不偏，用自己的心意去推想别人的心意，这种根本性的道理贯通所有事物始终。

传说在鲁国西部猎获了一只麒麟，孔子感叹朝廷传统的纲纪丧失，怨恨灾祸接连发生，饥荒连续不断。孔夫子的儒家学说在两千多年的历史发展中经历了荣辱兴废、岁月流逝、风风雨雨。孔子崇尚文化，兴办学校，具有开天辟地的意义，人们懂得了目标定位，福德善行源源不断地到来。能够养育我们的百姓，靠的是道理和教化，这只有孔子的学说才办得到，我们怎么能不认真遵循呢？

啊，我们的孔夫子十分圣明！他阐述先人之道，教育文化知识，引发人们的思想感情。孔子树立了最高的典范准则，他好比泰山之于山丘、河海之于水洼、麒麟之于走兽、凤凰之于飞鸟。自有人类以来，还没有全面超过孔子的，他是最突出优秀的。弟子守卫着他的学说，后来的学者继承遵守，汉朝和唐

祭孔大典现场　　　　　　（图片由济宁日报社提供）

The scene of Confucius Commemoration Ceremony.

朝的学者喜欢钻研章节字句的含义，宋朝和明朝的学者喜欢探讨儒家的大道理。儒家学说能够调和万物的和谐统一，从而使得物产丰富，人民安乐，孔子确实是历代的楷模，功劳与天地齐平。

浩大的道德风范，闪耀的儒家品行，仁爱诚信成为我们中华民族的精神品格。讲究信用，谋求和睦，国家得以安宁。近处的人们受到好处而喜悦，远方的人们也都闻风前来归附，到处都很和谐。道德制度规范，人心和顺，政事通达。修身、齐家、治国、平天下的优秀传统文化，一定会实现中华民族的伟大复兴。虔诚地祈祷孔夫子，一定要看到我们的真诚用心，保佑我们中国繁荣昌盛！

伏请您享用供品！

Text of the Dingyou Year (2017) Confucius Commemoration Ceremony

Writing team leader: Pan Lusheng

On the Gregorian Calendar, today is September 28, 2017. On the Chinese Lunar Calendar, it is the golden days of autumn in the Year of the Fire Rooster. On this day, on the Master's birthday, people from all walks of life, people with pious hearts and with great admiration for our departed sage— ritually gather together for the Commemoration Ceremony to honor and respect Confucius.

As it is written:

A legacy of brilliant civilization and style, the brilliant land of China, the land of the four Wise Emperors who created the laws codified by the Duke of Zhou.

It was from you that the Holy Master—great like the towering mountains—did come to promote righteousness, virtue, and correct behavior in accordance with the guidance of Heaven.

Putting together the lessons of the ancestors, editing and compiling the Six Classics, he set up the Apricot Altar and ushered in an age of flourishing thought, an age of benevolence, justice, propriety, and wisdom. Fair and righteous in his heart and moderate and virtuous in doing all things, respecting himself and respecting others, he understood that different perspectives result in different opinions.

Seeing his own actions as a metaphor for the collapse of discipline in society, it is said that—while on a hunting trip—Confucius wept when his arrow found its mark in a great and noble beast. Many were the natural disasters that struck one after another, and famine came upon the land.

A thousand years of honor and disgrace, a hundred generations of rising and falling, the stars turn in the heavens, and the dawn is about to break; people who labor outside without shelter from the wind and rain have a deep understanding of the world's needs.

Just as Pangu created order out of chaos, he advocated for literature and promoted education; knowing when enough is enough is the key to good fortune.

With principles and style, establish oneself as a servant of the people; this is the holy path, is it not?

Great Master, you are both holy and wise. Capable of understanding a text merely by looking at it, capable of explaining the meaning to your students.

A rare person with outstanding intelligence, you established norms and standards for upright behavior throughout the land. Three hundred years have passed since the Qing Emperor Yongzheng picked up his pen and wrote that future generations must always remember your supreme status in the creation of Confucian culture, and three hundred years more since the Ming Emperor Xianzong renovated your temple.

With disciples orbiting you like satellites around the North Star, every generation—Han, Tang, Song, and Ming—has recognized your preeminence.

Harmony between yin and yang brings prosperity to the people. A teacher of all ages shares the same merits as Heaven and Earth.

The sages' virtues—the bright light of Confucianism— have spread throughout the whole land. Benevolence and integrity are the soul of a people.

Whether between people or nations, it is important to maintain trust and seek harmony. When the country is at peace, the news of harmony will spread far and wide.

Just as straight lines cannot be used to make a circle, improper use of force cannot be used to correctly govern. Enlightened politics and proper morals are as necessary for the revival of China as self-cultivation, proper management of households and the land, and the appeasement and fulfillment of the common people's aspirations.

Sincerely, I pray to the Master! Sincerely, I ask him to protect China, and to help the nation prosper!

Please hear and respond to my prayers!

潘鲁生简介

潘鲁生：1962 年生，山东菏泽人，艺术学博士、教授，博士生导师，第十二届、十三届全国政协委员。现任中国文联副主席、山东省文联主席、山东工艺美术学院名誉院长，兼任中国民间文艺家协会主席、中国艺术研究院中国设计艺术院院长、中国国家画院院委、中国美术家协会工艺美术艺委会主任等职务。系中央联系的高级专家、享受国务院政府特殊津贴专家、全国宣传文化系统"四个一批人才"。

研究领域：艺术学、设计学和民艺学理论研究，长期从事设计教育与民间文艺保护实践。

主要著作：致力构建"民艺学"学科体系，著有《民艺学论纲》《设计论》《民间工艺学》《手艺农村》《美在乡村》等，主编《云冈纹饰全集》《手艺中国》等；从事艺术创作，作品《零的突破》《1997·破镜重圆》《葵花向阳》《延安——中国新文艺摇篮》等获多项荣誉。

Introduction to Pan Lusheng

Pan Lusheng, born in 1962 in Heze, Shandong Province, is a Doctor of Arts, professor, and doctoral supervisor. He is a member of the 12th and 13th National Committee of the Chinese People's Political Consultative Conference (CPPCC). Currently, he serves as the Vice Chairman of the Chinese Artists Association, Chairman of the Shandong Provincial Literary Federation, and Honorary Dean of the Shandong University of Art and Design. Additionally, he holds positions such as Chairman of the China Folk Literature and Art Association, President of the China Design and Art Institute, member of the China National Academy of Painting, and Director of the Art and Design Committee of the China Artists Association. He is recognized as a senior expert affiliated with the central government, enjoys a special subsidy from the State Council, and is recognized as one of the "Four Batches" of talents in the national publicity and cultural system.

Pan Lusheng's research focuses on theoretical studies in art, design, and folk art, with a long-standing commitment to design education and the preservation of folk arts.

His major works include efforts to establish the discipline of "folk art studies," with publications such as "Outline of Folk Art Studies," "Design Theory," "Folk Crafts

Studies," "Craftsmanship in Rural Areas," and "Beauty in the Countryside." He has also served as the chief editor of collections such as "The Complete Works of Yun Gang Ornamentation" and "Craftsmanship in China." In addition to his academic contributions, he is also an accomplished artist, with works such as "Breakthrough of Zero," "1997: Reunion of Broken Mirrors," "Sunflower Facing the Sun," and "Yan'an: Cradle of New Chinese Literature and Art," receiving numerous honors and awards.

2018 戊戌年
用儒家文化讲好中国故事

2018, the Year of Wuxu.
Telling China's stories with Confucian culture.

纪念孔子诞辰 2569 年

Commemorating the 2569th Anniversary of Confucius's Birth

戊戌（2018）年祭孔大典祭文

王志民　撰

维公元 2018 年 9 月 28 日，岁次戊戌，时序仲秋，至圣先师孔子诞辰 2569 周年之际，中华同胞、四海宾朋，同以诚敬之心，肃立大成殿前，谨奉鲜花乐舞，恭祭夫子及诸圣先哲。

其辞曰：

天地玄黄，宇宙洪荒；巍峨神州，屹立东方。
海岱[1]齐鲁，文明发祥；汶泗洙沂，源远流长。
春秋之季，乐坏礼崩；王道废弛，诸侯纷争。
天生仲尼，长夜启明；礼乐周鲁，玉汝于成。

创始儒学，体大思精[2]；远承尧舜，迩嗣周公。
仁礼忠信，孝悌中庸；崇德亲民，修齐治平。
华夏一体，大道之行；讲信修睦[3]，天下为公[4]。
杏坛设教，玉振金声；弟子三千，灿若辰星。

垂宪[5]后世，删述六经；文传八代，道承一统。

战国群雄，诸子争鸣；弘道[6]绪统，孟子荀卿。
秦汉六朝，薪火[7]传承；独尊儒术，三教汇通。
隋唐五代，西域东瀛；文播丝路，列国并迎。

宋明理学，大师辈涌；周程张邵，朱陆阳明。
道咸以降，中西交融；革故鼎新[8]，与时偕行。
千年儒脉，木铎声声；斯文在兹，乾清坤宁。
伟哉夫子，如日之明；同天并老，与世永恒。

改革开放，国运昌隆；不惑回首，气浩志宏。
机遇挑战，成竹在胸[9]；黾勉同心，众志成城。
百年目标，时代新命；求富图强，民族复兴。
寰宇一家，休戚与共；和而不同，合作共赢。

不负先哲，重任担承；不忘初心，勠力必成。
夫子之道，气贯长虹[10]；福佑中华，万世太平。
伏惟尚飨！

2018 年 9 月 28 日，时任山东省政协主席付志方恭读祭文。　　　（图片由济宁日报社杨国庆拍摄）

On September 28th, 2018, Fu Zhifang, Chairman of Shandong Provincial Political Consultative Conference at that time, solemnly recited the commemoration text.

◎ **注释**

1. 海岱：今山东省渤海至泰山之间的地带。海，渤海；岱，泰山。《书·禹贡》："海岱惟青州。"孔传："东北据海，西南距岱。"

2. 体大思精：规模宏大，构思精密。多指著作、设计规划等。南朝·宋·范晔《狱中与诸甥侄书》："此书行，故应有赏音者。纪传例为举其大略耳，诸细意甚多。自古体大而思精，未有此也。"明·胡应麟《诗薮·近体上》："李才高气逸而调雄，杜体大思精而格浑。"

3. 讲信修睦：讲究信用，睦邻修好。《礼记·礼运》："选贤与能，讲信修睦。"

4. 天下为公：原指君位不为一家私有，后为一种美好的社会政治理想。《礼记·礼运》："大道之行也，天下为公。"

5. 垂宪：垂示法则。《书·蔡仲之命》："尔乃迈迹自身，克勤无怠，以垂宪乃后。" 明·宋濂《使南稿序》："固当著之史牒，垂宪万世。"

6. 弘道：弘扬大道，弘扬正道。《论语·卫灵公》："人能弘道，非道弘人。"

7. 薪火：木柴虽有烧尽的时候，但火却可以传衍不息。比喻学术传授不绝。清·张通典《舜水先生祠落成敬赋》："薪火传姚江，遗书俟博访。"

8. 革故鼎新：《易·杂卦》："革，去故也；鼎，取新也。"后遂以"革故鼎新"指革除旧的，创建新的。

9. 成竹在胸：画竹子以前，心中先已有竹子的形象。宋·苏轼《文与可画筼筜谷偃竹记》："故画竹，必先得成竹于胸中。"后比喻处理事情之前心里早有通盘的考虑和打算。

10. 气贯长虹：形容气势壮盛，可以上贯长虹。老舍《老张的哲学》第十："酒菜上来，先猜拳行令，迎面一掌，声如狮吼，入口三杯，气贯长虹。"

◎ 译文

公元 2018 年 9 月 28 日，农历戊戌年，秋季的第二个月，是至圣先师孔子诞辰 2569 周年，中华同胞、四海宾朋，共同怀着诚敬的心情，肃立在大成殿前，谨奉鲜花和音乐舞蹈，恭敬地祭拜夫子和诸位圣人先哲。

祭文是：

天色玄地色黄，宇宙由混沌蒙昧逐渐开显之际；巍峨俊秀的神州大地，屹立在世界的东方。齐鲁拥有磅礴的大海和雄伟的泰山，是文明发祥之地；汶水、泗水、洙水、沂水，源远流长。春秋末年，乐坏礼崩；王道政治遭受严重践踏，各国诸侯纷争不断。上天生就孔子，犹如漫长的黑夜有了光明；一生为了恢复礼乐制度奔走呼号，在艰难困苦中成就自我。

开创体大思精的儒学思想，远承尧舜之道，近承周公之礼。倡导仁礼忠信，孝悌中庸；要求崇德亲民，修齐治平。华夏民族本是一家，大道通达无碍；讲求诚信、睦邻友好，以天下为公。在杏坛开讲，玉振金声；弟子三千，犹如辰星一般灿烂。

为后世垂示法则，删定阐述六经；文脉传衍不绝，大道一统传续。战国群雄纷争，诸子百家争鸣；释为"弘扬继承孔子学说"的有孟子、荀子。秦朝汉朝南北六朝，薪火传承；汉武帝独尊儒术，儒释道三教汇通。隋朝唐朝五代，西域日本都受到儒家文化的影响；儒家文化随着丝绸之路传播开来，西域列国并相欢迎。

宋明理学，出现了周敦颐、程颢、程颐、张载、邵雍、朱熹、陆九渊、王阳明这些儒学大师。清朝道光咸丰以来，中西文明交融；儒家学术也革故鼎新，与时偕行。千年的儒学文脉，仍旧发挥着它的重要作用；正是因为儒家文化，天朗气清、国泰民安。伟大啊夫子，像太阳一样光明；与天不老，与世永恒。

改革开放以来，国运昌隆；回顾四十年来的波澜历程，气势浩大，志向恢宏。机遇和挑战并存，但百年复兴的梦想成竹在胸；大家努力勤奋，团结一心，众志成城，必当成就大业。

祭孔大典现场 （图片由济宁日报社提供）

The scene of Confucius Commemoration Ceremony.

两个一百年奋斗目标，谋求国家富强，百姓安居乐业，中华民族的伟大复兴，是新时代的使命。全球一家，休戚与共；和而不同，合作才能共赢。

不辜负先哲，勇于承担重任；不忘记初心，齐心协力便能成功。夫子的思想，气贯长虹；福佑着中华大地，万世太平。

伏请您享用供品！

Text of the Wuxu Year (2018) Confucius Commemoration Ceremony

Written by: Wang Zhimin

On the Gregorian Calendar, today is September 28, 2018. On the Chinese Lunar Calendar, it is the middle of autumn in the Year of the Earth Dog. Two thousand, five hundred and sixty-nine years have passed since the birth of our Master Confucius. Now, with sincere respect, Chinese compatriots, guests, and friends from all over the world stand together solemnly in front of the Dacheng Hall. In paying homage to the Master and all the sages, I would like to offer flowers, music, and dance.

With these words:

The sky and the Earth are mysterious; the universe is vast, and the land of China is majestic.

Shandong's mountains and ocean are the progenitors of civilization; her great rivers flow a long way.

In the waning years of the Spring and Autumn Period, proper observance of music and ritual was abandoned; the king's might was lax due to negligence, and the marquises were revolting.

Bringing light to the darkness of the long night, it was to this environment that Confucius was born; through training, he came to understand the rites and music of the land.

With a strong body and a clever mind, he founded Confucianism and inherited the wisdom of both the Duke of Zhou and the mythical emperors Yao and Shun.

Be benevolent, courteous, loyal, and trustworthy; engage in filial piety and practice moderation in all things; be virtuous and close to the people; cultivate the self; manage well your family and country; and appease the common people's aspirations in the world.

On a journey on the great road of time, China and her people are one; keep faith and cultivate harmony, and all things in the world will serve the common good.

He set up the Apricot Altar, used bells to make sounds, chimes to complete rhythms, and passed on profound knowledge; he had three thousand disciples, each as bright as the stars in the sky.

Editing and compiling the Six Classics for the benefit of future generations; cultural knowledge passes from parent to child and child to grandchild for all eternity.

During the Warring States period, all the heroes and scholars contended, and Mencius and Xunzi helped carry forward his fine traditions and morality.

During the Qin, the Han, and the Six Dynasties, a spark was lit and passed down; only Confucianism could braid the three Great Religions together.

In the Sui, Tang, and Five Dynasties, it spread to the Western Regions and Japan; it spread along the Silk Road, and all countries welcomed it.

The Neo-Confucianism of the Song and Ming dynasties was full of great masters: Zhou Dunyi, Cheng Hao, Zhang Zai, Shao Yong, Zhu Xi, Lu Xiangshan, and Wang Yangming.

From the reigns of the Qing Emperors Daoguang and Xianfeng (1820-1861) onward, there has been an ever-growing fusion between the Orient and the Occident, reforming the old, creating the new, and keeping pace with the changing times!

After thousands of years of inheritance, the chimes still ring as pure as always; great things still trace their origins to Confucianism, the heavens are clear, the country is peaceful, and the people are safe.

Great Master, you are as bright as the sun at noon; you are eternally great, and the words of praise in honor of you that have been passed down from generation to generation will be passed down for countless generations yet to come.

Reform and opening up have brought prosperity to the country; looking back at the road traveled, we can see the grand vigor that brought success.

Seizing opportunities and challenges with a confident mind, working hard with an indomitable unity of will.

The Centenary Goals are the times' new destiny: seeking wealth and strength and the great rejuvenation of the Chinese people.

We are one world; we share both weal and woe and harmoniously accept others' differences in search of peaceful development and win-win cooperation.

Live up to the ideals of the sages and shoulder important responsibilities; do not forget our earliest intentions, and work hard to achieve success.

The Master's Way is like a rainbow; bless China for prosperous and peaceful times throughout all ages.

I respectfully beseech you!

王志民简介

王志民：1948 年生，山东淄博人，现任山东师范大学特聘资深教授、博士生导师，山东理工大学特聘教授，教育部重大课题攻关项目"稷下学派文献整理与数据库建设研究"首席专家；国家文化公园专家委员会成员，尼山世界文明论坛学术委员会副主任，历任中国孟子研究院特聘院长、山东理工大学齐文化研究院院长等。

研究领域：中国古代文学尤其是齐鲁古代文学研究，齐鲁文化特别是齐文化研究。

主要著作：出版《齐文化概论》《齐文化论稿》《齐文化与鲁文化》《稷下散思——齐鲁古代文学简论》《齐鲁文化概说》《齐鲁文化与中华文明》《序论齐鲁文化》《先秦儒学与齐鲁文化》等 11 部专著，发表论文 100 余篇。对齐鲁文化的形成渊源、内在结构、精神特质以及与中华文明的关系进行了系统、深入的研究，提出了比较完备的理论阐释体系和创新性见解，对儒学与齐文化关系做了开拓性研究。

Introduction to Wang Zhimin

Wang Zhimin, born in 1948 in Zibo, Shandong Province, currently serves as a distinguished professor and doctoral supervisor at Shandong Normal University, as well as a distinguished professor at Shandong University of Science and Technology. He is also the chief expert of the major project "Compilation of Jixia School Literature and Construction of Database Research" under the Ministry of Education. Additionally, he is a member of the National Cultural Park Expert Committee and the Vice Chairman of the Academic Committee of the Nishan World Civilization Forum. Wang Zhimin has previously served as the dean of the Chinese Mencius Research Institute and the dean of the Qilu Cultural Research Institute at Shandong University of Science and Technology.

His research primarily focuses on ancient Chinese literature, especially the study of ancient literature in the Qi and Lu regions, as well as the research of Qi culture, particularly in relation to Chinese civilization.

His major works include "Introduction to Qi Culture," "Essays on Qi Culture," "Qi Culture and Lu Culture," "Reflections on Jixia: A Brief Introduction to Ancient Literature in the Qi and Lu Regions," "Overview of Qi and Lu Culture," "Qi and Lu Culture and Chinese Civilization," "Introduction to Qi and Lu Culture," and "Pre-Qin Confucianism and Qi and Lu Culture," among others. He has published over 100 papers, conducting systematic and in-depth research on the origins, internal structure, and spiritual characteristics of Qi and Lu culture, as well as its relationship with Chinese civilization. He has proposed a comprehensive theoretical interpretation system and innovative insights, pioneering research on the relationship between Confucianism and Qi culture.

2019 己亥年
用儒家文化讲好中国故事

2019, the Year of Jihai.
Telling China's stories with Confucian culture.

纪念孔子诞辰2570年

Commemorating the 2570th Anniversary of Confucius's Birth

己亥（2019）年祭孔大典祭文

郭齐勇　撰

维公元二〇一九年九月廿八日，先师孔子诞降二千五百七十年，中华人民共和国成立七十周年前夕，社会各界贤达齐集洙泗弦歌之地，万仞宫墙之内，圣庙丹墀之下，谨以心香之忱，芳菲之芯，伴以八佾之舞、清庙[1]之乐，恭祭先师孔子在天之灵，辞曰：

华夏文明，源远流长。榛莽[2]开辟，艰苦备尝。
聚族而居，德性陶养。安土敦仁，大爱无疆。
启沃[3]族群，厥为圣王。羲娲炎黄，尧舜禹汤。
文武周公，蹈厉发扬[4]。方策[5]布列，元典高张。

迄吾夫子，木铎天降。少陈俎豆，礼容端庄。[6]
长肄文献，私学开讲。弟子三千，济济一堂。
周游列国，栖栖遑遑。不合世用，退立纪纲。
手定六经，启下承上。金声玉振[7]，大成克当。

深体天心，鉴观圣王。发明仁学，人道允彰。

欲仁仁至，大本在卬。己立立人，忠心坦荡。
不欲勿施，恕情深长。格致诚正，修身乃臧。
家齐国治，咸宁万邦。爱及万类，钓而不纲[8]。

和谐宇宙，生机洋洋。圣教垂统，禹域同光。
陶铸君子，温良恭让。文明以止[9]，四裔[10]风向。
寰球大通，远播影响。西哲服膺，万国崇仰。
德慧渊广，要在仁让。身心以宁，人伦偕畅。

2019 年 9 月 28 日，时任山东省委常委、常务副省长王书坚恭读祭文。（图片由济宁日报社杨国庆拍摄）

On September 28th, 2019, Wang Shujian, Member of the Standing Committee of the CPC Shandong Provincial Committee and Executive Vice Governor of Shandong Province at that time, solemnly recited the commemoration text.

小康将成，大同可望。保合天地，万类繁昌。

天人物我，勿失勿忘。大中至正，人类绵长。

今我中华，盛大气象。建国七秩，涅槃凤凰。

民族复兴，传统尊尚。礼敬圣贤，福佑未央。

泰山苍苍，洙泗泱泱。夫子之风，山高水长。

肃肃 ¹¹ 祗祗 ¹²，格于形上 ¹³。先师有灵，伏惟尚飨！

◎ 注释

1. 清庙：（1）《诗·周颂》篇名。《诗·周颂·清庙序》："《清庙》，祀文王也。"（2）指古帝王祭祀祖先的乐章。《礼记·乐记》："《清庙》之瑟，朱弦而疏越，壹倡而三叹。"《尚书大传》卷二："古者帝王升歌《清庙》之乐。"郑玄注："《清庙》，乐章名。"（3）太庙。古代帝王的宗庙。《诗·周颂·清庙》："於穆清庙，肃雝显相。"《左传·桓公二年》："是以清庙茅屋……昭其俭也。"《文选·司马相如〈上林赋〉》："登明堂，坐清庙。"郭璞注："清庙，太庙也。"

2. 榛莽：杂乱丛生的草木。

3. 启沃：《书·说命上》："启乃心，沃朕心。"孔颖达疏："当开汝心所有，以灌沃我心，欲令以彼所见，教己未知故也。"后因以"启沃"谓竭诚开导、辅佐君王。

4. 蹈厉发扬：本指舞蹈时动作的威武。《礼记·乐记》：

"发扬蹈厉，大（太）公之志也。"孔颖达疏："言武乐之舞，发扬蹈厉象大（太）公威武鹰扬之志也。"《史记·乐书》："发扬蹈厉之已蚤，何也？"张守节正义："发，初也。扬，举袂也。蹈，顿足蹋地。厉，颜色勃然如战色也。"后用以形容精神奋发，意气昂扬。

5. 方策：简册，典籍。后亦指史册。《礼记·中庸》："哀公问政。子曰：'文武之政，布在方策，其人存，则其政举；其人亡，则其政息。'"郑玄注："方，版也。策，简也。"孔颖达疏："言文王、武王为政之道皆布列于方牍简策。"

6. 少陈俎豆，礼容端庄：《史记·孔子世家》："孔子为儿嬉戏，常陈俎豆，设礼容。"孔子小时候做游戏，常常摆起各种祭器，学做祭祀的礼仪动作。

7. 金声玉振：《孟子·万章下》："孔子之谓集大成。集大成也者，金声而玉振之也。金声也者，始条理也；玉振之也者，终条理也。始条理者，智之事也；终条理者，圣之事也。"孟子以音乐演奏为比喻，说明孔子是一位集大成的先贤。

8. 钓而不纲：指夫子用鱼竿钓鱼而不用渔网捕鱼。论语·述而》："子钓而不纲，弋不射宿。"

9. 文明以止：《易·象》："刚柔交错，天文也；文明以止，人文也。"

10. 四裔：（1）指幽州、崇山、三危、羽山四个边远地区。因在四方边裔，故称。语出《书·舜典》："流共工于幽州，放驩兜于崇山，窜三苗于三危，殛鲧于羽山。"按，孔传，幽州，北裔；崇山，南裔；三危，西裔；羽山，东裔。《左传·文公十八年》："舜臣尧，宾于四门，流四凶族，浑敦、穷奇、梼杌、饕餮，投诸四裔，以御螭魅。"（2）指四方边远之地。汉·班固《西都赋》："原野萧条，目极四裔。"明·宋应星《天工开物·白瓷》："若夫中华四裔，驰名猎取者，皆饶郡浮梁、景德镇之产也。"

11. 肃肃：恭敬貌。《诗·大雅·思齐》："雝雝在宫，肃肃在庙。"毛传："肃肃，敬也。"

12. 祗祗：恭敬貌。《书·康诰》："庸庸祗祗，威威显民。"

13. 形上：无形；抽象。《易·系辞上》："是故形而上者谓之道，形而下者谓之器。"

◎ 译文

公元二〇一九年九月廿八日，先师孔子诞辰二千五百七十年，中华人民共和国成立七十周年前夕，社会各界的贤达聚集在洙泗弦歌的地方，在万仞宫墙之内，圣庙丹墀之下，以真诚的心意，香美的祭品，伴随着八佾之舞、清庙之乐，恭敬地祭祀先师孔子在天之灵，祭文是：

华夏文明源远流长，从草木丛生中开辟，备尝艰苦。聚族而居，培养造就了道德的本性。安心于土地，崇尚人与人相亲相爱的无限的大爱。伏羲、女娲、炎帝、黄帝、尧、舜、禹、商汤开导族群，成为圣王。周文王、周武王、周公旦精神焕发，意气昂扬，为政之道布列在方牍简策，施设形成了古代的典章。

孔子是上天派来教化人群的木铎。小时候做游戏，常常摆起各种祭器模拟祭祀，礼仪端庄。成年后学习古代文献，开讲私学。弟子三千，济济一堂。孔子周游列国宣扬理想，整日匆忙奔走，政治主张不为诸侯所用，回到鲁国后整理典籍，阐述治理国家的根本法度。亲自删定六经，在中华文化中发挥了承上启下的作用。孔子的智慧与德行仿佛金声玉振，是古代文化的集大成者。

深切体会天心，观察圣王，发明阐发仁学，彰显人道的重要性。根本在于自己，我想达到仁，仁就到了。仁者之心是推己及人，自己想要自立，也帮助别人自立。心胸开朗，真诚坦率。自己不愿意的事，不强加于别人，推己及人，意味深长。获得知识，真诚意念，修养自身的品性。管理好自己的家庭和

祭孔大典现场　　　　　　　（图片由济宁日报社提供）

The scene of Confucius Commemoration Ceremony.

家族，治理好自己的国家，万邦和谐安宁。将这种仁爱的思想推及自然万物，用鱼竿钓鱼而不用渔网捕鱼。

宇宙间充满了和谐与生机，文化传统得以传承，整个国家繁荣昌盛。培养君子，具备温良恭俭让的品质。文明而有节制，四方的民族都向往和学习。环球交流沟通，产生了深远的影响。西方的哲学家也对此表示敬佩和折服，受到世界各国的尊敬和仰慕。道德和智慧的深远影响，关键在于仁爱和谦让。这使得我们的身心和谐安宁，人与人之间的关系更加融洽顺畅。

我们即将建成小康社会，大同世界也期望达成。保持自然和谐，万物繁荣昌盛。博大精深的中和之道最为公正，人类得以延续不断。如今，我们中华拥有盛大的气象，新中国成立70年取得了辉煌的成就。民族复兴成为我们的共同追求，尊重传统成为人们的共识。对古代道德才智杰出的哲人表达尊崇，福祉无尽绵长。

泰山郁郁苍苍，洙泗水流深广，夫子之风如山高如水长。让我们怀着肃穆恭敬的心情，向先师表达最崇高的敬意，先师在天有灵，伏请您享用供品！

Text of the Jihai Year (2019) Confucius Commemoration Ceremony

Writen by: Guo Qiyong

On the Gregorian Calendar, today is September 28, 2019. It is the 2,570th anniversary of the birth of our great teacher, Confucius. On the eve of the 70th anniversary of the founding of the People's Republic of China, talented people from all sectors of society have gathered at the confluence of the Zhu and Si rivers, at the temple in front of the south gate of Qufu's City Walls. With sincerity in their hearts, they stand beneath the eaves of the holy temple, as fragrant incense wafts its way skyward, and their worship of the spirit of our ancestor Confucius in Heaven is accompanied by sixty-four dancers and the music of the temple.

It has been said:

Chinese civilization has a long history. Opening up the desolate wilderness and enduring hardships.

Cultivated similar morals and virtues, birds of a feather flock together. Once people's hearts are at peace, they will naturally be kind-hearted, and they will naturally be able to use their benevolent hearts to transform society and purify people's hearts. Boundless love sees no distinction in terms of country, region, or race but instead respects all people with a tolerant mind and without asking for anything in return.

Part of the group who wholeheartedly dedicated themselves to the enlightenment and assistance of rulers, he was a gentleman among gentlemen and the sage of sages. Fu-Hsi and Nü-wa created humanity, music, hunting, fishing, and cooking, and the four Wise Emperors (Tang Yao, Yu Shun, Xia Yu, and Shang Tang) created government.

The Duke of Zhou inherited these governmental ideals and vigorously promoted them. Occupying a high position, the political theories of King Wen and King Wu are recorded in the Classics.

The Master recognized the warning chimes sounded by Heaven. Polite and dignified, he followed ritual and etiquette.

After studying for a long time, he eventually began to teach. One school produced 3,000 disciples.

Busy and restless, he traveled around the land. Not fit for the quotidian world, he retired from public life in search of a way to establish discipline.

Inheriting the past and opening up the future, he compiled the "Six Classics." Showing profound knowledge and the ability to learn well, he was able to take on great responsibility.

Deeply embodying Heaven's benevolence, I honor our holy Master. Creator of the philosophy of benevolence, manifesting humanitarianism.

To be kind and benevolent starts from a correct foundation. To improve others, one must first improve oneself. Improving oneself begins with loyalty and magnanimity.

Follow the Golden Rule. Don't do to others what you don't want them to do to you. Forgive transgressions against the self. Sincerity, integrity, and self-cultivation are the way.

Home and country must be orderly and well-governed for all parties to achieve tranquility. Benevolence is not limited to one's fellow man but also the birds, beasts, and the environment.

A harmonious universe is filled with vitality. Passed from

ancient times to future generations, all of China is illuminated by Confucianism's holy light.

The lathe of Heaven is what refines a person into a courteous and virtuous gentleman. Since the beginning of civilization, the winds of change have blown across the land.

Throughout the globe, his influence has spread far and wide. Admired by all nations, even Western philosophers have learned from him.

Benevolence is based on virtue and wisdom. Peace in mind and body ensures harmonious relationships.

A moderately prosperous society will be achieved, and the achievement of the Great Harmony is to be looked forward to. Protect the balance of Heaven and Earth, and all types of things shall prosper.

Heaven's gifts must not be lost nor forgotten. One should be neutral, benevolent, and righteous; one should focus on tranquility and act to establish humanity until the end of time.

Today's China is growing ever grander. With an indomitable spirit and a promising future, seventy years have passed since the founding of the People's Republic.

The great rejuvenation of the Chinese people requires respecting tradition. Pay homage to the sages, and blessings are sure to come.

Mount Tai is green and lush, and the Zhu and Si rivers flow peacefully. The Master's style is as imposing as the tall mountains and as endless as the rivers.

With a solemn and respectful manner, I address the spirit of our departed Master, and I beseech you to answer my prayers!

郭齐勇简介

郭齐勇：1947年生，湖北武汉人，哲学博士，武汉大学哲学学院教授，博士生导师；兼任武汉大学学术委员会委员暨人文学部学术分委员会主任、国学院院长、中国传统文化研究中心名誉主任、孔子与儒学研究中心主任；国家社会科学基金哲学学科评审组专家、国际中国哲学会副执行长、中国哲学史学会副会长、中华孔子学会副会长。

研究领域：中国哲学史的教学与研究，专长儒家哲学与20世纪中国哲学，国家重点学科"武汉大学中国哲学学科"学术带头人。

主要著作：专著《中国哲学史》《中国儒学之精神》《现当代新儒学思潮研究》《中国哲学智慧的探索》《中华人文精神的重建》《儒学与现代化的新探讨》《熊十力哲学研究》《熊十力传论》《郭齐勇自选集》《文化学概论》《守先待后：文化与人生随笔》，合著《诸子学通论》《梁漱溟哲学思想》《钱穆评传》《传统氤氲与现代转型》等，主编《熊十力集》《中国古典哲学名著选读》《当代中国哲学研究》《中国哲学史经典精读》《儒家文化研究》辑刊等。

Introduction to Guo Qiyong

Guo Qiyong, born in 1947 in Wuhan, Hubei Province, is a Ph.D. in Philosophy and a professor at the School of Philosophy at Wuhan University, where he also supervises doctoral students. He holds various positions, including member of the Academic Committee and Director of the Academic Sub-Committee of the Faculty of Humanities at Wuhan University, Dean of the Institute of Chinese Studies, Honorary Director of the Center for Research on Traditional Chinese Culture, and Director of the Confucius and Confucianism Research Center. Additionally, he serves as an expert in the Philosophy Discipline Review Group of the National Social Science Foundation, Vice Executive Director of the International Society for Chinese Philosophy, Vice President of the Chinese Society for the History of Philosophy, and Vice President of the Chinese Confucius Association.

His research focuses on the teaching and research of the history of Chinese philosophy, with expertise in Confucian philosophy and 20th-century Chinese philosophy. He is the academic leader of the national key discipline "Chinese Philosophy" at Wuhan University.

Guo Qiyong's major works include "History of Chinese Philosophy," "The Spirit of Chinese Confucianism," "Research on Contemporary Neo-Confucianism Trends," "Exploration of the Wisdom of Chinese Philosophy," "Reconstruction of Chinese Humanistic Spirit," "New Exploration of Confucianism and Modernization," "Research on Xiong Shili's Philosophy," "Essays on Xiong Shili's Transmission," "Selected Works of Guo Qiyong," "Introduction to Cultural Studies," and "Waiting First and Waiting Later: Essays on Culture and Life." He has also co-authored works such as "Introduction to the Study of the Masters," "Philosophical Thought of Liang Shuming," "Biography and Critique of Qian Mu," and "Traditional Nebulosity and Modern Transformation." Furthermore, he has edited collections such as "Collected Works of Xiong Shili," "Selected Readings of Classical Chinese Philosophy," "Research on Contemporary Chinese Philosophy," "Classic Readings in the History of Chinese Philosophy," and "Studies on Confucian Culture."

2020 庚子年
全球云祭孔

2020, the Year of Gengzi.
Global Online Commemoration of Confucius

纪念孔子诞辰 2571 年

Commemorating the 2571st Anniversary of Confucius's Birth

庚子（2020）年祭孔大典祭文

王学典　撰

公元二零二零年九月二十八日，岁在庚子，时维仲秋，值至圣先师孔子 2571 年诞辰，华夏儿女、四海高朋肃聚于曲阜孔庙大成殿前，秉至诚之忱，怀敬仰之情，谨备清酒时果、雅乐佾舞，敬奠夫子及诸鸿儒贤哲之灵。其辞曰：

大哉夫子，万世之师！天命木铎，玉振金声！
雍雍[1]穆穆[2]，昭德[3]丕明。诗书既定，礼乐遂成。
令闻令望，生民物轨[4]。先觉先知[5]，桃李滋盛[6]。
酌彼金罍[7]，其香始升[8]；钟鼓和鸣，天人是听。

昔我古初，丧乱弘多[9]。鸿蒙[10]未辟，大道不行。
尧舜汤武，厥功兴替。周室倾颓，尾大[11]相征。
惟怀逮愍[12]，黎民如沸[13]。嗟我夫子，陬鲁以生。
少能事鄙[14]，壮也志弘。立仁以礼，允乎大成。

复礼兴乐，博文[15]克难。周游既厄，化雨杏坛。

诲人不倦，七十二贤。有教无类，弟子三千。
斯文在兹，道济¹⁶ 乾坤。删述¹⁷ 六经，郁郁乎文。
实天生德，高山景行¹⁸。己立立人¹⁹，众星拱辰。

伟哉夫子，遗泽万世！孟轲缵绪²⁰，荀卿继踵²¹。
汉兴唐承，以启宋明。哲人济济，以昌以隆。
伟哉中华，薪火相递！外邦扰攘，我自承平。
时虽遇疫，众志成城。嗣我至圣，永安永宁！
泰山岩岩，荫佑我邦；不维山高，仁义丕显！

2020 年 9 月 28 日，时任山东省委副书记、省长李干杰恭读祭文。（图片由济宁日报社杨国庆拍摄）

On September 28th, 2020, Li Ganjie, Deputy Secretary of the CPC Shandong Provincial Committee and Governor of Shandong Province at that time, solemnly recited the commemoration text.

洙泗涣涣，流泽我疆；岂维河广，圣人德衍！
文圣斯恒，华夏学宗。上继前圣，下启太平！
仁爱无涯，德充苍穹。嗣圣孔子，天下大同！
典祀有常，雅乐声扬。育我胶庠[22]，保我家邦！
伏惟尚飨！

◎ 注释

1. 雍雍：声音和谐。《礼记·少仪》："鸾和之美，肃肃雍雍。" 汉·蔡邕《祖饯祝》："鸾鸣雍雍，四牡彭彭，君既升舆，道路开张。"

2. 穆穆：端庄恭敬。《书·舜典》："宾于四门，四门穆穆。"《尔雅·释训》："穆穆，敬也。"

3. 昭德：（1）明德；美德。《国语·郑语》："唯荆实有昭德，若周衰，其必兴矣。" 汉·刘向《说苑·善说》："天有昭德，宝鼎自至。"（2）汉代雅舞名。汉文庙奏《昭德》《文始》《四时》《五行》之舞。见《汉书·礼乐志》。

4. 生民物轨：生民，人民。宋·佚名《大晟府拟撰释奠十四首》："百王宗师，生民物轨。"《书·毕命》："道洽政治，泽润生民。" 物轨，众人的榜样。《晋书·文苑传·李充》："圣人之在世，吐言则为训辞，莅事则为物轨。"

5. 先觉先知：指对事物发展的认识早于一般人。《孟子·万章上》："天之生此民也，使先知觉后知，使先觉觉后觉也。"

6. 滋盛：众多；兴旺。《后汉书·翟酺传》："孝宣论六经于石渠，学者滋盛，弟子万数。"

7. 酌彼金罍：《诗·国风·周南·卷耳》："我姑酌彼金罍，维以不永怀。"

8. 其香始升：《诗·大雅·生民》："其香始升，上帝居歆。"

9. 丧乱弘多：弘多，甚多。《诗·小雅·节南山》："天方荐瘥，丧乱弘多。"

10. 鸿蒙：宇宙形成前的混沌状态。《庄子·在宥》："云将东游，过扶摇之枝，而适遭鸿蒙。"成玄英疏："鸿蒙，元气也。"

11. 尾大：比喻臣下势力强大。《后汉书·王充王符仲长统列传》："疏禁厚下，以尾大陵弱。"李贤注："言周室微弱而诸侯强盛，如尾大然。"

12. 惟怀逮愍：《晋书·儒林传序》："惟怀逮愍，丧乱弘多，衣冠礼乐，扫地俱尽。"

13. 如沸：《诗·大雅·荡》："如蜩如螗，如沸如羹。"

14. 少能事鄙：鄙事，鄙人之事。旧多指各种技艺与耕种等体力劳动。《论语·子罕》："吾少也贱，故多能鄙事。"何晏集解引包咸曰："故多能为鄙人之事。"

15. 博文：指通晓古代文献。《论语·雍也》："君子博学于文，约之以礼。"

16. 道济：用道德行为影响、教育。《易·系辞上》："与天地相似，故不违。知周乎万物，而道济天下，故不过。"

17. 删述：是指删减述作，即对古代文献进行删减和整理，以便更好地传承和教授。这里的"六经"指的是中国古代的六部经典著作，包括《诗》《书》《礼》《易》《乐》《春秋》。

18. 高山景行：语出《诗·小雅·车辖》："高山仰止，景行行止。"高山，比喻高尚的德行。景行，大路，比喻行为正大光明。后以"高山景行"比喻崇高的德行。

19. 己立立人：自己立身从而使他人立身。《论语·雍也》："己欲立而立人，己欲达而达人。"

20. 缵绪：继承世业。明·刘基《尊闻堂铭》："卓彼圣哲，有开于先，弘猷秩昭，缵绪维贤。"

21. 继踵：接踵，前后相接。《史记·范雎蔡泽列传》："及二人羁旅入秦，继踵取卿相。"南朝·梁·刘勰《文心雕龙·杂文》："自《七发》以下，作者继踵。"唐·胡曾《咏史诗·五湖》："不知范蠡乘舟后，更有功臣继踵无？"

22. 胶庠：周代学校名。周时胶为大学，庠为小学。后世通称学校为"胶庠"。《礼记·王制》："周人养国老于东胶，养庶老于虞庠。"

◎ 译文

公元 2020 年 9 月 28 日，农历庚子年，仲秋时节，在至圣先师孔子 2571 年诞辰，华夏儿女、来自四海的贵宾庄严肃穆地聚集在曲阜孔庙大成殿前，怀着真诚的心意和敬仰之情，准备好了清酒和时令果品，以及祭祀的乐舞，恭敬地祭奠孔子和诸位大儒贤哲。祭文是：

伟大的孔子啊，很多代人的老师！上天降下的宣扬教化的人，学问以敲钟为开始，以击磬为结尾。端庄恭敬，美德显明。整理编订《诗经》《尚书》作为教材，形成以礼为社会秩序，以乐和合天下的文化思想。您美好的声望，是众人的榜样。对事物发展的认识早于一般人，培养了很多门生弟子，他们都成为了贤才。向您敬献祭酒，祭典上香烟缭绕，钟鼓和鸣，天人能听到。

在我国的太古时期，经历了很多丧亡和乱世。世界混沌，治理的原则没有施行。尧、舜、商汤、周武王等上古和三代的先王，在统治的盛衰更迭中，完成了伟大的功业。到周朝将要灭亡的时候，诸侯相互征讨，人民好像生活在沸水中。这时孔子在鲁国陬邑出生，年轻时贫贱，所以多能鄙事，壮年时志趣宏大。用仁和礼作为人群相处的道理和制度，集中国古代传统文化之大成。

恢复和兴起礼乐，广学汇通一切人文的典章制度、著作义理，克服困难。孔子周游列国，遭遇困厄，回到鲁国，兴办教育，有三千弟子，七十二贤人。对所有的人给予教育，不区分类别，教导别人不知疲倦。文化在这里，用道德行为影响和教育人民大众。删减整理《诗》《书》《礼》《乐》《易》《春秋》六经，礼乐仪制富盛。德行崇高，自己立身从而使他人立身，孔子如同众星拱卫的北极星。

孔子多么伟大，给万世留下德泽。孟子继承了他的儒学事业，荀子也紧随其后。汉朝兴起，唐朝继承，宋朝又发扬光大。人才众多，儒学昌隆。伟大的中华，薪火相传。外邦扰乱，我国治平相承。现在虽然遭遇疫情，我们众志成城，共同抗击疫情。延续孔子的精神，永远安定太平！

泰山高耸，护佑着我们的国家。不仅山高，而且昭显着仁义。洙水和泗水水流盛大，泽被我国的疆域，不止是河水广阔，而是像圣人的道德一样在绵延。文化圣人孔子长长久久，是华夏文化的创始人。上继承以前的圣人，往后开启了我国社会的太平。仁爱没有边际，道德充满天空。延续圣人孔子的精神，天下趋向大同。祭祀合乎礼仪规范，雅乐声音高扬。开启了我国的平民教育，安定了我们的国家。请接受我们对您的崇敬，伏请您享用供品！

祭孔大典现场　　　　　　（图片由济宁日报社提供）

The scene of Confucius Commemoration Ceremony.

Text of the Gengzi Year (2020) Confucius Commemoration Ceremony

Written by: Wang Xuedian

On the Gregorian Calendar, today is September 28, 2020. On the Chinese Lunar Calendar, it is the middle of autumn in the year of the Gold Rat. On the occasion of the 2571st birthday of our most holy teacher, Confucius, sons and daughters of the Chinese nation and distinguished friends from all over the world have gathered solemnly in front of the Dacheng Hall of the Confucius Temple in Qufu. With sincerity and admiration, I would like to pay homage to the spirit of the Master and other great scholars and sages. Thus, I have prepared wine and fruit and elegant music and dance. As it is written:

Great Master, teacher of all ages! Heaven's warning bell rang out loud and announced the profound knowledge he had to share!

Harmonious and dignified, a virtuous and inspiring role model. Compiling not only poems and books, he also finalized rituals and music.

Admired and imitated by all, he was the model for the people and all living things. Preaching enlightenment and knowledge, and the fruit of his labor as a teacher takes root across the land.

Filling the golden pot with fragrant wine whose aroma fills the whole sanctuary, bells, and drums chime in harmony, and Heaven listens.

In the earliest times, chaos was still upon the land.

There was a time before order was created.

During the time of the mythical Emperors Yao and Shun, the Shang Dynasty was followed by the Xia Dynasty.

As the Zhou Dynasty declined, vassals grew in power. The lack of virtue and fighting among the mighty affected the common people.

It was to this place and time that the Master was born in Zou, born in Shandong.

Humble in his youth, he had great ambitions.

Establishing the philosophy of benevolence and propriety, he achieved great success.

Reviving the proper observance of ritual and music, he overcame many difficulties. After a period spent roaming the land, he established the Apricot Altar.

Tireless in teaching, he was followed by the Seventy-Two Sages. Three thousand in number, his disciples knew that the things which one can be educated in are without limit.

Great things and people trace their origins to Confucianism. Editing and compiling the Six Classics and making a wealth of knowledge available.

Born of Heaven, his virtues are as magnificent as mountains.

Teaching the creed that the prerequisite to improving yourself is to help improve others, he was orbited by students like satellites around the North Star.

Great Master, your legacy will last forever! Followed in turn by Xunzi then by Mencius. Your thought prospered in the Han Dynasty, and helped the Tang Dynasty flourish. Throughout the Song and Ming dynasties scholars and scholarship helped the nation prosper.

You are the spark that lit the fire. As times of trouble affect the outside world, you have brought us calm and assurance.

Although the world is struck with epidemic disease, we have an indomitable unity of will.

As heirs to your most holy philosophy, we can know peace and tranquility!

The craggy Mount Tai protects our country, our home, and our family; no matter how difficult the challenge is, benevolence and righteousness will be revealed!

How can it be that the Zhu and Si rivers flow so far and so wide?

How can it be that our sage is so awesome and virtuous?

Eternal literary sage, you are the founder of Chinese philosophy.

Inheritor of fine traditions, teacher of great ways!

Benevolence has no boundaries; virtue fills the vastness of the sky.

Praising you with proper sacrifices and solemn ceremonies, praising you to the sound of elegant music, we ask you as the creator of the philosophy that has taught us benevolence and virtue to protect us, protect our home, and protect our country!

Of this, I respectfully beseech you!

王学典简介

王学典： 1956 年生，山东滕州人，第十四届全国政协常委，第六届国际儒学联合会副会长、山东大学儒学高等研究院执行院长，中国农民战争史学会理事长、中国史学会史学理论研究分会副会长、中国墨子学会副会长、全国高等学校文科学报研究会副理事长、中国经济社会理事会第五届理事会理事等。

研究领域： 史学理论及史学史研究、中国现代学术文化史研究，尤长于中国现当代史学思想及史学思潮研究。

主要著作： 出版《历史主义思潮的历史命运》《二十世纪后半期中国史学主潮》《20 世纪中国史学评论》《翦伯赞学术思想评传》《顾颉刚和他的弟子们》等多部学术专著，主编《史学引论》《述往知来——历史学的过去、现状与前瞻》。其中，《顾颉刚和他的弟子们》在知识界赢得较高声誉，而《二十世纪后半期中国史学主潮》一书则被普遍认为是近 50 年中国史学史研究的拓荒之作，为海内外同行所瞩目。在《中国社会科学》《历史研究》《近代史研究》《北京大学学报》《文史哲》等重要期刊上发表论文 90 余篇，在学术界产生了相当的影响力。

Introduction to Wang Xuedian

Wang Xuedian, born in 1956 in Tengzhou, Shandong Province, currently serves as a member of the 14th National Committee of the Chinese People's Political Consultative Conference (CPPCC). He is also the Vice President of the 6th International Confucian Association and the Executive Dean of the Institute of Confucian Studies at Shandong University. Additionally, he holds positions such as Chairman of the Chinese Association for the History of the Farmer's War, Vice President of the Historical Theory Research Branch of the Chinese Historical Society, Vice President of the Chinese Mozi Society, Vice Chairman of the Research Society of Humanities and Social Sciences in Higher Education Institutions, and Member of the 5th Council of the Chinese Economic and Social Council.

His research areas include historical theory and the history of historiography, as well as the study of Chinese modern academic and cultural history. He is particularly adept at researching the intellectual trends and currents in modern and contemporary Chinese historiography.

Wang Xuedian's major works include "The Historical Destiny of Historicism," "Mainstream Trends in Chinese Historiography in the Latter Half of the 20th Century," "Reviews of Chinese Historiography in the 20th Century," "A Biographical Study of Gu Jiegang's Academic Thought," and "Gu Jiegang and His Disciples," among others. He has also edited "Introduction to Historiography" and "Reflecting on the Past and Looking Forward: Past, Present, and Future of Historical Studies." "Gu Jiegang and His Disciples" has received significant acclaim in intellectual circles, while "Mainstream Trends in Chinese Historiography in the Latter Half of the 20th Century" is widely regarded as a pioneering work in the study of Chinese historiography over the past 50 years, attracting attention from scholars both at home and abroad. Wang Xuedian has published over 90 articles in prestigious journals such as "Social Sciences in China," "Historical Research," "Research on Modern History," "Journal of Peking University," and "Wenshi Ziliao," exerting considerable influence in the academic community.

2021 辛丑年
礼序乾坤　乐和天地

2021, the Year of Xinchou.
Etiquette orders the universe, and harmony fills heaven and earth.

纪念孔子诞辰2572年

Commemorating the 2572nd Anniversary of Confucius's Birth

辛丑（2021）年祭孔大典祭文

王钧林　撰

维公元二〇二一年九月二十八日，岁次辛丑，时序仲秋，天覆地载，寰球一家，凡我中华暨世界各地人士于兹孔子诞辰之日而诣至阙里[1]孔庙大成殿前者，谨以虔诚崇敬之心，庄严肃穆之礼，敦和美盛之乐，致祭于至圣孔子之灵，配以复圣颜子、宗圣曾子、述圣子思子、亚圣孟子。祝曰：

泰山岩岩[2]，黄河汤汤[3]。金风吹万[4]，乾坤清朗[5]。
尼山苍苍，洙泗洋洋。钟灵毓圣，海宇瞻望。
永锡木铎[6]，祗承天贶[7]。生民未有，师表无双。
缵绪[8]尧舜，仪型文王[9]。圣集大成，万世景仰。

天道民彝[10]，有纲有常。天纵其才，美德阐扬。
博施济民，仁爱无疆。质直[11]好义，君子道长。
修己以敬[12]，恭俭礼让。崇德辨惑，智慧深广。
躬行忠信，作孚万邦[13]。行久有恒，载芬载芳。

始终条理[14]，思想宝藏。仰之弥高，万仞宫墙。
允执厥中[15]，无偏无党。正直公平，王道荡荡。
同则不继[16]，和能丰长。和而不同，文明发皇[17]。
肇造乐土，赋我理想。远慕大同，近奔小康。

先知先觉，制作宪章[18]。允文允武，治国安邦。
为政以德，北辰取象[19]。成人成己，两美并扬。
修道讲学，日就月将。牖世觉民[20]，缉熙[21]重光。
首出庶物[22]，万民向往。巍乎成功，焕乎文章。

2021 年 9 月 28 日，时任山东省委副书记、省长李干杰恭读祭文。 （图片由济宁日报社杨国庆拍摄）

On September 28th, 2021, Li Ganjie, Deputy Secretary of the CPC Shandong Provincial Committee and Governor of Shandong Province at that time, solemnly recited the commemoration text.

乃彝乃训[23]，式遵[24]不忘。乃绳乃矩[25]，肯构肯堂[26]。

宅兹中国[27]，与有荣光。景运[28]维新，介福[29]延祥。

天下和平，民迪安康[30]。顺天应人[31]，复兴在望。

吾土吾民，再造辉煌。告慰夫子，爰荐馨香。

尚飨！

◎ 注释

1. 阙里：孔子故里。在山东曲阜城内阙里街。因有两石阙，故名。孔子曾在此讲学。后建有孔庙，几占全城之半。《孔子家语·七十二弟子解》："颜由，颜回父，字季路，孔子始教学于阙里，而受学，少孔子六岁。"

2. 岩岩：高大、高耸的样子。《诗·鲁颂·閟宫》："泰山岩岩，鲁邦所詹。"孔颖达疏："言泰山之高岩岩然，鲁之邦境所至也。"

3. 汤汤：水流浩大湍急的样子。《书·尧典》："汤汤洪水方割，荡荡怀山襄陵，浩浩滔天。"孔传："汤汤，流貌。"《诗·卫风·氓》："淇水汤汤，渐车帷裳。"毛传："汤汤，水盛貌。"

4. 金风吹万：金秋时节，风吹万窍，发出天籁般的声音。金风，秋风；万，万窍。《庄子·齐物论》："夫吹万不同，而使其自己也。"成玄英疏："风唯一体，窍则万殊。"

5. 乾坤清朗：天地清净明亮。乾坤，指天地。

6. 永锡木铎：永久赐给人类木铎。锡，同"赐"。木铎，木舌的铜铃铛。手摇铃铛，使木铎敲击铃铛发出响声。《论语·八佾》："天下之无道也久矣，天将以夫子为木铎。"意思是上天将以孔子作为代言人。

7. 祗承天贶：恭敬承接上天的恩赐。祗，恭敬。贶，赐予。阮籍《通易论》："昭明其道，以答天贶。"

8. 缵绪：继承世业，特指君主继位。

9. 仪型文王：以周文王为典范。仪型，楷模、典范。《诗·大雅·文王》："仪刑文王，万邦作孚。"刑，通型。

10. 民彝：人伦纲常。《书·康诰》："天惟与我民彝。"孔传："天与我民五常，使父义、母慈、兄友、弟恭、子孝。"

11. 质直：朴实正直。《论语·颜渊》："夫达也者，质直而好义。"刘宝楠《论语正义》："谓达者之为人，朴质正直，而行事知好义也。"

12. 修己以敬：恭敬谨慎，自我修养。《论语·宪问》："修己以敬"。

13. 作孚万邦：天下邦国都信服。作孚，信服、信从。《诗·大雅·文王》："仪刑文王，万邦作孚。"

14. 始终条理：有始有终，逻辑清晰。《孟子·万章下》："孔子之谓集大成。集大成也者，金声而玉振之也。金声也者，始条理也；玉振之也者，终条理也。始条理者，智之事也；终条理者，圣之事也。"

15. 允执厥中：公允、平实地秉持中正的立场与原则。《书·大禹谟》："人心惟危，道心惟微。惟精惟一，允执厥中。"后世将其概括称为道统十六字心传。

16．同则不继：雷同的事物不能生长延续。《国语·郑语》："夫和实生物，同则不继。以他平他谓之和，故能丰长而物生之。"

17．发皇：发达兴盛。

18．宪章：法度、典章制度。

19．北辰取象：取用北辰之象。《论语·为政》："为政以德，譬如北辰，居其所而众星共之。"

20．牖世觉民：照亮社会，觉醒民众。牖，室与堂之间的窗子，透过窗子照进阳光。觉，觉醒。

21．缉熙：光明、光辉。《诗·大雅·文王》："穆穆文王，於缉熙敬止。"毛传："缉熙，光明也。"又，《诗·周颂·敬之》："日就月将，学有缉熙于光明。"郑玄笺："缉熙，光明也。"

22．首出庶物：首，始。庶，众。源源不断创生万事万物。《周易·乾卦》："保合太和，乃利贞。首出庶物，万国咸宁。"

23．乃彝乃训：你的法度你的训诫。彝，法度、常规。训，训诫。

24．式遵：遵守。式，发语词。

25．乃绳乃矩：你的绳墨你的规矩。绳，绳墨，引申为法度、标准。矩，规矩。

26．肯构肯堂：肯构造肯建堂，意指能够遵照先人的设计建造新的堂屋。明·董其昌《容台文集》卷七《尘隐居士像赞》："其志则洁，其行则芳。乃绳乃矩，肯构肯堂。"

27. 宅兹中国：居此中国。何尊铭文："余其宅兹中国，自兹乂民。"

28. 景运：大运。意指改革开放的国运。

29. 介福：大福。《周易·晋卦》："受兹介福，于其王母。"

30. 民迪安康：民众进至安康。迪，至，进。

31. 顺天应人：顺应天命，合乎人心。《易·革》："天地革而四时成。汤武革命，顺乎天而应乎人，革之事大矣哉。"孔颖达疏："殷汤周武，聪明睿智，上顺天命，下应人心。"

◎ 译文

公元二〇二一年九月二十八日，农历辛丑年仲秋时节，天覆地载，寰球一家，凡我中华暨世界各地人士在孔子诞辰日来到阙里孔庙大成殿前，以虔诚崇敬的心情、庄严肃穆的礼节、敦和美盛的音乐，祭拜至圣孔子的在天之灵，配以复圣颜子、宗圣曾子、述圣子思子、亚圣孟子。祭文是：

泰山巍峨高耸，黄河奔流浩荡。秋风吹拂，天地清朗。尼山松柏苍苍，洙泗河水洋洋。天地凝聚灵气孕育了圣人，海内外各界人士为之仰望。夫子是上天赐予人间的代言人，我们虔诚地接受上天的恩赏。夫子出类拔萃，自人类产生以来从未有过，为人师表举世无双。继承和发展了尧舜事业，以周文王为楷模榜样。集先圣之大成，备受万世景仰。

天道有纲，人伦有常。夫子以其卓绝的天赋之才，致力于美德的阐明与宣扬。博施于民而济众，夫子之仁，大爱无疆。质朴正直，崇尚道义，君子之道日益上长。个人修养严肃谨慎，做到恭敬、节俭、礼让。推崇道德，辨析困惑，智慧既深且广。践行忠信，天下邦国无不信服向往。仁义礼智信持之以恒，行之有常，必能带来人间的芬芳。

思维缜密深邃，自始至终，条理清晰，成为人类的思想宝藏。越仰望越觉得崇高，犹如不可逾越的万仞高墙。主张秉持中正之道，不结党，无偏向。正直公平，王道平坦宽广。雷同的事物不能生生不息，不同类别的事物和合在一起才能创新生长。遵循和而不同的规律，人类文明才会含弘光大，昂扬直上。构造人间乐土，赋予民众理想。远则钦慕天下大同，近则盼望实现小康。

夫子先知先觉，为人类社会制作法度宪章。能文能武，治国安邦。为政崇尚道德，正身正己，譬如北极星为众星所环绕一样。人人交好，互相成就，成人成己，两美并扬。修道讲学，天天努力进取，月月积极向上。照亮世间，开启民智，点燃光明之光。推陈出新，不断构建新法度新目标，不断创生新理念新思想，引得万民向往。立功不朽，崇高伟大；立言不朽，璀璨有章。

夫子的法度与训诫，一体遵守不忘。夫子的绳墨与规矩，一体继承发扬。居此中国，无上荣光。国家的命运在于维新，大福祉延续大吉祥。天下和乐太平，人民幸福安康。顺应时代潮流与人民心愿，民族复兴可见可望。我们的国家、我们的人民，必将再次创造新的辉煌。为告慰夫子的在天之灵，谨奉上几缕祭品馨香。

伏请您享用供品！

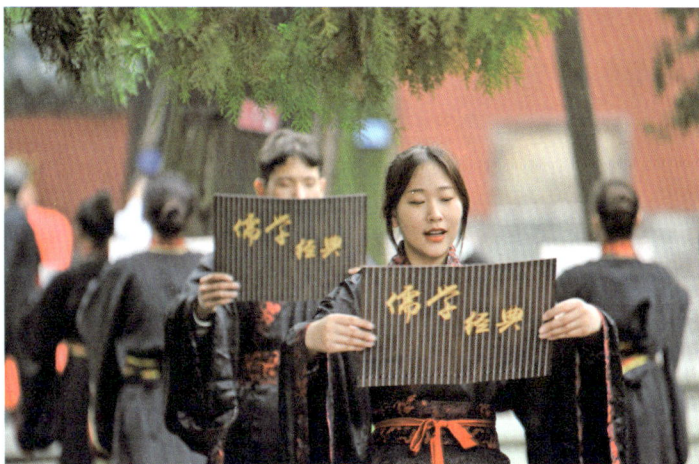

祭孔大典现场 　　　　　（图片由济宁日报社提供）

The scene of Confucius Commemoration Ceremony.

Text of the Xinchou Year (2021) Confucius Commemoration Ceremony

Written by: Wang Junlin

On the Gregorian Calendar, today is September 28, 2021. On the Chinese Lunar Calendar, it is the middle of autumn in the Year of the Gold Ox. The sky covers everything, and the Earth bears everything. The whole world is one family. On this day, this anniversary of the birth of Confucius, guests from China and from places all over the world have come to the Dacheng Hall in Qufu's Confucius Temple. Standing in front of the temple, sincerely reverent, with solemn etiquette and harmonious and beautiful joy, we offer sacrifices to the spirit of the most holy Confucius and to his most holy students, Yan Hui, Zengzi, Sizi, and Mencius.

Blessings:

From the craggy boulders of Mt. Taishan to the roiling waters of the Yellow River, the pure autumn breeze blows throughout the whole world.

Nishan is green and lush. The Zhu and Si rivers flow to the sea.

The beautiful mountains and rivers and numerous sages born of this land are far-seeing and wise.

A wise and filial child hears Heaven's warning bells and is comforted by them.

Three hundred years have passed since the Qing Emperor Yongzheng picked up his pen and wrote that future generations must always remember your supreme status in the creation of Confucian culture, for you are an unparalleled teacher.

Carrying on the traditions of the Mythical Emperors Yao and Shun, following the standards of King Wen of Zhou.

The great works you compiled have been admired by all generations and will be admired by all generations yet to come.

Resulting in order and orderliness, Heaven's Way provides ethical and moral principles for how people should get along with each other.

Favored by Heaven, you demonstrated and publicized the concepts of virtue.

Benevolence to the people, benevolence without bounds, teaching that a man of integrity and righteousness is a gentleman.

You said to cultivate yourself with respect, and be respectful, thrifty, and courteous. Your wisdom of advocating virtue and discerning doubts is both profound and broad.

Act faithfully, and all nations will prosper. Perseverance means the ability to turn beautiful dreams into beautiful reality.

Organized from start to finish, your ideology is a treasure trove.

Gathered at the temple in front of the south gate of Qufu's City, we recognize that the longer we investigate your principles, the greater we realize they are.

Impartial in words and deed, no party or faction is favored over any other one. Adhering to integrity and fairness, a ruler should not be swayed by petty factions.

Life is born from differences, but harmony shall lead to prosperity. A flourishing civilization and harmony for all parties do not require uniformity.

To create a paradise requires ideals. In the hopes of eventually achieving the Great Harmony, we currently strive for a moderately prosperous society in all respects.

Understanding things before the rest of us, you laid out a path for us to follow.

Capable of describing both civil and military, you helped stabilize the nation and ensure peace.

A ruler who governs with virtue and morality is steady and unwavering, like the North Star. To achieve self-actualization, one must also assist others. Virtue does not exist in a vacuum.

Improve, practice, teach, and study, and the months will pass as days do. With education, the people of the world are inspired to open their eyes and look around them.

All people and all things experience both coming and going, alpha and omega. How majestic the accomplished works! How glorious instituted regulations!

We will not forget to follow the teachings and admonishments given by our forefathers to our descendants.

The rules and standards that govern us have been passed from father to son and son to grandson.

Modern-day China will find glory, restoration, blessings, and good fortune.

The world beneath Heaven is peaceful, and the people of the world are healthy. If we follow Heaven's law and respond to the needs of the common man, revival is within our sights.

For our land and our people, we can once again create glory.

Comforted by my Master's teachings, I offer incense and praise.

And I do humbly beseech you!

王钧林简介

王钧林：1956 年生，山东莱阳人，曲阜师范大学特聘教授，孔子文化研究院院长，山东师范大学齐鲁文化研究院教授，山东省大舜文化研究会会长，国际儒学联合会理事，中国孔子基金会理事、学术委员。先后担任《齐鲁学刊》《海岱学刊》《孔子研究》主编。1996 年被评为山东省专业技术拔尖人才，享受国务院特殊津贴。2016 年被聘为孔子研究院特聘专家、尼山学者，2017 年被评为山东省泰山产业领军人才。

主要研究领域：儒学与中国历史文化。

主要著作：出版《山东通史·先秦卷》《门外说儒》《中国儒学史·先秦卷》《儒学的知识、思想与智慧》《斯文在兹——儒学与中国传统文化》等多部著作，发表重要学术论文数十篇，主持并完成国家社科基金课题"17—20 世纪中国孔教运动研究"、教育部人文社科重点研究基地重大项目"儒家哲学与现代文明"等，多次获得山东省社会科学优秀成果一等奖和重大成果奖。

Introduction to Wang Junlin

Wang Junlin, born in 1956 in Laiyang, Shandong Province, is a distinguished professor at Qufu Normal University, where he also serves as the Director of the Confucius Culture Research Institute. He is also a professor at the Qilu Institute of Culture at Shandong Normal University and the President of the Da Shun Culture Research Association in Shandong Province. Additionally, he is a director of the International Confucian Association and a member of the Board and Academic Committee of the Confucius Foundation of China. Wang Junlin has previously served as the chief editor of journals such as "Qilu Academic Journal," "Haidai Academic Journal," and "Confucius Research." In 1996, he was honored as a top professional and technical talent in Shandong Province and received a special government subsidy from the State Council. In 2016, he was appointed as a special expert and Nishan Scholar at the Confucius Institute, and in 2017, he was recognized as a leading talent in the Taishan industry in Shandong Province.

His primary research focuses on Confucianism and Chinese historical and cultural studies.

Wang Junlin has authored several significant works, including "General History of Shandong: Pre-Qin Volume," "Beyond the Door: Confucianism," "History of Chinese Confucianism: Pre-Qin Volume," "Knowledge, Thought, and Wisdom of Confucianism," and "Sculpting Civilization: Confucianism and Traditional Chinese Culture," among others. He has published dozens of important academic papers and has led and completed major research projects funded by the National Social Science Foundation and the Ministry of Education's Key Research Base for Humanities and Social Sciences. He has received numerous first prizes and major achievement awards for social science research in Shandong Province.

2022 壬寅年
仁礼天下　和合大同

2022, the Year of Renyin.
Benevolence and ritual govern the world, achieving great unity.

纪念孔子诞辰
2573
年

Commemorating the 2573rd Anniversary of Confucius's Birth

壬寅（2022）年祭孔大典祭文

鲍鹏山　撰

维公元二〇二二年九月二十八日，岁在壬寅，时属仲秋，值至圣先师孔子诞辰 2573 年，华夏儿女、四海宾朋，敬拜于曲阜阙里[1]孔子庙大成殿前，秉至诚敬仰之心，谨备蔬果鲜花，献以礼乐佾舞[2]，敬告夫子及诸圣哲、贤儒之灵。其辞曰：

宇宙洪荒，华夏泱泱；盘古开天，爰及三皇。

五帝肇基，夏禹更张；文武周公，缵绪商汤。

甲骨钟鼎，文明之光；诗书礼乐，王道荡荡[3]。

平王东迁，周室苍惶；明王不作，诸侯恣狂。

攻伐失序，伦理无章；礼坏乐崩，斯文将亡。

圣王之道，何堪其殇；三代之统，栖栖遑遑。

东鲁有人，出类拔萃；天生仲尼，长夜清光。

志学不惑，知命从心；[4]存亡继绝，六经阐扬。

礼别乐和，宽裕温良；春秋继诗，窃议朝堂。

布衣定制，天下咸往；诸侯卿相，平治垂裳。

夫子大成，万世慕仰；教化人伦，于斯立方。

诗书不传，庠序[5]废坠；杏坛设帐，学以大昌。

修齐治平，立心立命；君子之儒[6]，宽厚自强[7]。

志道据德，依仁游艺；[8]从容中道[9]，内圣外王[10]。

有教无类，万仞门墙；延及后世，文脉绵长。

大哉孔子，道冠古今；伟哉圣人，德业发皇。

郁郁文哉[11]，礼乐华章；护佑华夏，瓜瓞[12]无疆。

迨及当代，其命维新[13]；允富允教[14]，乃隆乃彰。

汇通中西，百虑同归[15]；远来近悦[16]，迭用柔刚[17]。

天下一家，四海咸辉；命运与共，协和万邦[18]！

伏惟尚飨！

2022 年 9 月 28 日，山东省委副书记、省长周乃翔恭读祭文。 （图片由济宁日报社杨国庆拍摄）

On September 28th, 2022, Zhou Naixiang, Deputy Secretary of the CPC Shandong Provincial Committee and Governor of Shandong Province, solemnly recited the commemoration text.

◎ 注释

1. 阙里：孔子故里。在山东曲阜城内阙里街。因有两石阙，故名。孔子曾在此讲学。后建有孔庙，几占全城之半。《孔子家语·七十二弟子解》："颜由，颜回父，字季路，孔子始教学于阙里，而受学，少孔子六岁。"

2. 佾舞：乐舞。佾，舞列。八佾舞，纵横都是八人，古代天子用的一种乐舞。《论语·八佾》："孔子谓季氏，八佾舞于庭，是可忍也，孰不可忍也！"朱熹集注："佾，舞列也；天子八，诸侯六，大夫四，士二。"

3. 王道荡荡：遵循先王正道而行。《书·洪范》："无偏无党，王道荡荡。"《论语·泰伯》："大哉尧之为君也……荡荡乎，民无能名焉。"朱熹集注："荡荡，广远之称也。"

4. 志学不惑，知命从心：《论语·为政》："子曰：吾十有五而志于学，三十而立，四十而不惑，五十而知天命。"

5. 庠序：古代的地方学校。后亦泛称学校。《孟子·梁惠王上》："谨庠序之教，申之以孝弟之义。"

6. 君子之儒：君子式的儒者。《论语·雍也》："女为君子儒，无为小人儒。"清·弘历《学古堂》："欲识圣人道，应为君子儒。"

7. 宽厚自强：《易·乾》："天行健，君子以自强不息。"《易·坤》"地势坤，君子以厚德载物。"

8. 志道据德，依仁游艺：以道为志向，以德为根据，以仁为依靠，以艺为游憩。《论语·述而》："子曰：'志于道，据于德，依于仁，游于艺。'"

9. 从容中道：《礼记·中庸》："诚者，不勉而中，不思而得，从容中道，圣人也。"孔颖达疏："从容闲暇而自中乎道。"

10. 内圣外王：古代修身为政的最高理想。谓内备圣人之至德，施之于外，则为王者之政。《庄子·天下》："是故内圣外王之道，暗而不明，郁而不发，天下之人，各为其所欲焉，以自为方。"《宋史·道学传一·邵雍》："河南程颢初侍其父识雍，论议终日，退而叹曰：'尧夫，内圣外王之学也。'"

11. 郁郁文哉：《论语·八佾》："周监于二代，郁郁乎文哉！吾从周。"邢炳疏："郁郁，文章貌。"郁郁，文采盛貌。

12. 瓜瓞：喻子孙繁衍，相继不绝。《诗·大雅·文王之什·绵》："绵绵瓜瓞，民之初生，自土沮漆。"朱熹集传："大曰瓜，小曰瓞。瓜之近本初生常小，其蔓不绝，至末而后大也。"

13. 其命维新：《诗·大雅·文王》："周虽旧邦，其命维新。"毛传："乃新在文王也。"陈奂传疏："维，犹乃也；维新，乃新也……言周至文王而始新之。"维新，乃始更新。

14. 允富允教：《论语·子路》："冉有曰：'既庶矣，又何加焉？'曰：'富之。'曰：'既富矣，又何加焉？'曰：'教之。'"后以"富教"指富民和教民。谓使人民富裕，并加以教育。

15. 百虑同归：使各种不同的思想归于一致。《易·系辞下》："天下同归而殊涂，一致而百虑。"

16. 远来近悦：近居的人悦服，远处的人慕化而来。形容政治清明，远近归附。《论语·子路》："叶公问政，子曰：'近者说，远者来。'"邢炳疏："子曰：当施惠于近者，使之喜说，则远者当慕化而来也。"

17. 迭用柔刚：《易·说卦》："昔者圣人之作《易》也，将以顺性命之理。是以立天之道曰阴与阳，立地之道曰柔与刚，立人之道曰仁与义。兼三才而两之，故《易》六画而成卦。分阴分阳，迭用柔刚，故《易》六位而成章。"或柔或刚更相为用，故曰"迭"。

18. 协和万邦：《书·虞书·尧典》："克明俊德，以亲九族；九族既睦，平章百姓；百姓昭明，协和万邦。"

◎ 译文

公元 2022 年 9 月 28 日，农历壬寅年，仲秋时节，值至圣先师孔子诞辰 2573 年，华夏儿女、来自四海的宾朋，恭敬地站在曲阜阙里孔庙大成殿前，秉持着诚恳敬仰的心，准备蔬果、鲜花、祭祀乐舞，纪念孔子、历代的思想家。祭文是：

宇宙莽莽苍苍，中华大地广阔。盘古开天辟地，到三皇五帝肇始基业，夏禹变更革新，周文王、周武王继承了夏、商。商周的甲骨文、金文，文明光辉灿烂。诗书礼乐，遵循先王正道而行宽广浩荡。周平王东迁，周王室衰微，没有贤明的君主，诸侯肆意作为，无所顾忌。诸侯国之间攻打讨伐，秩序混乱，失去伦理失去了次序。制度和规范遭到破坏，文化和道德即将废弃。

圣贤先王之道怎能忍受就此夭亡。夏、商、周三代的典章制度、礼仪教化无处安放。鲁国出现了卓越出众的圣人孔子，如同漫长的黑夜中出现了光明。孔子立志求学，明辨是非，知晓事物规律，遇事从心所欲。阐明发扬《诗》《书》《礼》《乐》《易》《春秋》六经，使受到损坏的中华传统文化得以继续存在延续。用礼立德安民，用乐凝聚人心，用温良宽厚使人民喜爱。《春秋》继承了《诗经》的主旨，对朝廷政事进行褒贬议论。孔子以一介布衣之力制定了制度规范，为天下人认可遵从。各诸侯王和执政的大臣依据孔子的仁礼施政。

祭孔大典现场　　　　（图片由济宁日报社提供）

The scene of Confucius Commemoration Ceremony.

　　孔子集圣贤的大成得到万世的仰慕，形成教化人伦的基本理念。春秋官学衰败，孔子创办私学，在杏坛聚徒授业讲学，带来学问昌盛。君子践行儒家的行为，既重视自身修养又有安定国家的政治抱负，既顺应天道又涵养道德，既宽大厚道又努力图强。志向在道上，据守在德上，依靠在仁上，游憩在艺上。自然合乎道，内备圣人之德，外施王者之政。不论贵贱贤愚都给以教育，道德学问高深莫测，对后世影响深远，文化源远流长。

　　孔子思想多么伟大，从古至今引导着人们的行为。中华传统文化相继不绝，中华的繁荣昌盛代代绵延。到了当代更加焕发华彩，人民富裕，人民教育更加兴盛。融合中西，使各种不同的思想归于一致。政治清明，远来近悦，外交刚柔并济，天下人如一家人，世界各国共同繁荣，命运与共，和睦相处，友好和谐。

　　伏请您享用供品！

Text of the Renyin Year (2022) Confucius Commemoration Ceremony

Written by: Bao Pengshan

On the Gregorian Calendar, today is September 28, 2022. On the Chinese Lunar Calendar, it is the middle of autumn in the Year of the Water Tiger. On the occasion of the 2573rd birthday of our most holy teacher, Confucius, sons and daughters of China and friends from all over the world gather to worship in front of the Dacheng Hall in Qufu's Confucius Temple. With sincere respect, we have prepared offerings of fruits and flowers and expressions of etiquette, music, and dance as a way of giving thanks to the spirit of the Master and all the sages and Confucian philosophers. In these words:

The universe is vast and unending. China is enormous; Pangu created the heavens and Earth, and his wisdom passed through the generations until the era of the Three Emperors, the creation of agriculture and ritual.

The Five Great Rulers established the foundation; Yu the Great Engineer was even more powerful; the governmental ideals inherited by the Duke of Zhou were the same as the ones that governed the Shang and the Xia.

Oracle bones, bells, and tripods, the light of civilization, poetry, books, rituals, music, and the unswerving integrity of kings.

As the rule of the Zhou collapsed and the kings were subverted by their underlings, they were forced to move eastwards; if the king did not act, what could the rest of the world do to fight against hegemony and oppression?

Attacks against order led to ethical disorder. Proper observance of ritual and music was neglected, and civilized behavior fell by the wayside.

In such a deplorable situation, what could one do?

Inheritor of the Xia, Shang, and Zhou, Holy Confucius traveled the land seeking a wise ruler with whom he could illuminate the darkness of the long night.

Determined to learn without confusion, know destiny, follow his heart, and restore the destroyed country, he promoted the Six Classics to the people.

Courtesy, joy, harmony, generosity, and gentleness: his words were promoted throughout the Spring and Autumn Period.

Even though they are not leaders, the common man still cares about the state of the world and yearns for world peace; princes, dukes, ministers, and kings have the responsibility to seek peace and prosperity for their subjects.

The wonders of the great Master have been admired by all generations; he taught enlightenment via the idea that human relations should be based on filial piety and respect for teachers.

When poems and books were not being passed down, and academies were collapsing, he set up the Apricot Altar from which he taught.

Establish your mind and destiny by cultivating the self, managing your family and country well, and appeasing the common people's aspirations in the world; generosity and self-reliance are the markers of a Confucian scholar and a gentleman.

Aspire to the truth of the Tao, and base your actions on virtue; choose benevolence, calmly follow the middle path, be a saint on the inside and a king on the outside.

At the Wanren Temple in front of the Gates of Qufu, there is a place where one can be educated in more things than countable; born of history, this cultural thread will extend to the ends of time.

How great is Confucius, the Master of ancient and modern times! How great is Confucius, the holy saint with awesome virtue and amazing achievements!

His gorgeous rhetoric, rich and colorful, protects the countless descendants of the Chinese people.

Entering the contemporary era, his destiny has been renewed; as the people find prosperity, they come to seek further knowledge.

Connecting China and the West, all considerations lead to the same goals; the achievement of this is good news that will be spread both far and wide.

The world is one family, shining brightly; we share a common destiny for harmony among all nations!

I respectfully beseech you!

鲍鹏山简介

鲍鹏山：1963 年生，安徽六安人，民革党员，文学博士，作家，学者；上海开放大学人文学院教授，青海师范大学硕士研究生导师，上海交通大学兼职教授；中国作家协会会员，中国孔子基金会学术委员会委员。央视《百家讲坛》、上海电视台《东方大讲坛》、上海教育电视台《世纪大讲坛》、山东教育卫视《新杏坛》等栏目的主讲嘉宾。

研究领域：中国古代文学、古代文化的教学与研究。

主要著作：出版《〈论语〉导读》、《后生小子——诸子百家新九章》、《附庸风雅——第三只眼看〈诗经〉》、《历史的多维透视》、《中国人的心灵：三千年理智与情感》、《鲍鹏山新读诸子百家》、《诸子百家新读》（与刘德水先生合著）以及《彀中英雄》、《天纵圣贤》、《绝地生灵》、《孔子传》（中国青年出版社出版）等著作 30 多部。全国多家杂志的专栏作者，作品被选入多种文集及人民教育出版社的全国统编高中语文教材。

Introduction to Bao Pengshan

Bao Pengshan, born in 1963 in Luan, Anhui Province, is a member of the Revolutionary Committee of the Chinese Kuomintang, a Ph.D. in literature, writer, and scholar. He serves as a professor at the Academy of Humanities at Shanghai Open University, a master's supervisor at Qinghai Normal University, and a part-time professor at Shanghai Jiao Tong University. He is also a member of the China Writers Association and a member of the Academic Committee of the Confucius Foundation of China. He has appeared as a keynote speaker on programs such as CCTV's "Lecture Room of Hundred Schools," Shanghai TV's "Great Lecture Hall of the East," Shanghai Education TV's "Century Lecture Hall," and Shandong Education Satellite TV's "New Apricot Platform." His research focuses on ancient Chinese literature and the teaching and research of ancient culture.

His major works include over 30 publications, such as "An Introduction to the Analects," "Posthumous Youngsters: A New Nine Chapters of Hundred Schools," "Adhering to Elegance: Viewing the Book of Songs with a Third Eye," "A Multi-Dimensional Perspective of History," "The Soul of the Chinese: Three Thousand Years of Reason and Emotion," "Bao Pengshan's New Reading of the Hundred Schools," "New Readings of the Hundred Schools" (co-authored with Mr. Liu Deshui), "Heroes in the Gorge," "Heaven's Gifted Saints," "Survivors in Desolation," and "Biography of Confucius" (published by China Youth Publishing House). He also contributes columns to various national magazines, and his works have been selected for numerous anthologies and included in the national curriculum for high school Chinese language textbooks published by People's Education Press.

2023 癸卯年

盛世华章　和合大同

2023, the Year of Guimao.
In this prosperous era, let harmony prevail, achieving great unity.

纪念孔子诞辰
2574
年

Commemorating the 2574th Anniversary of Confucius's Birth

癸卯（2023）年祭孔大典祭文

王　杰　撰

维公元 2023 年 9 月 28 日，岁次癸卯，时在仲秋，值先师诞辰 2574 周年之际，华夏贤达、四海宾朋、孔子后裔，谨以鲜花雅乐敬献于曲阜孔庙大成殿前，恭祭先师孔子、四配及诸贤哲。其辞曰：

大哉中华！
茫茫九州，亘古洪荒；日月并耀，辰宿列张。
万物并育[1]，不悖道常；与民更始[2]，五帝三皇。
允执厥中[3]，尧舜禹汤；夙夜在公[4]，文武成康。

圣哉仲尼！
尼山嶙峋，洙水曲邑。夫子诞降，麟趾呈祥。
择善[5]思齐[6]，君子有方；一以贯之[7]，以仁为上。
诗书教化，六艺弥彰；因材施教，师道荡荡。

伟哉夫子！
忠信[8]孝悌[9]，务本[10]守常；礼序乐和，大同小康。
四时行焉，百物生长；流谦[11]处顺[12]，文脉悠长。

经世致用，内圣外王；譬如北辰[13]，万古同光。

壮哉神州！
百年变局，风起云扬；四海乂安，五洲激荡。
谁谓河广？一苇能杭[14]；岁不我与[15]，大道康庄。
守正创新，自信自强；亲仁善邻[16]，协和万邦。

盛哉儒学！
中华文明，源远流长；时代益新，文化日昌。
"两创"并举，殷殷瞩望；"两个结合"，指明方向。
斯文在兹，其道大光；于今为盛，再谱华章。

2023 年 9 月 28 日，山东省委副书记、省长周乃翔恭读祭文。 （图片由济宁日报社陈硕拍摄）

On September 28th, 2023, Zhou Naixiang, Deputy Secretary of the CPC Shandong Provincial Committee and Governor of Shandong Province, solemnly recited the commemoration text.

恭敬至哉，夫子如在！

钟鼓渊渊，琴瑟铿锵；金声玉振，响彻四方。

氤氲满庭，穆穆在堂¹⁷；高山仰止，心驰神往。

旧邦新命¹⁸，功崇业广¹⁹。佑我华夏，百世祯祥。

虔肃献供，伏惟尚飨！

◎ 注释

1. 并育：共同生长。《礼记·中庸》："万物并育而不相害，道并行而不相悖。"

2. 与民更始：与百姓一道去旧立新。《汉书·武帝纪》："朕嘉唐虞而乐殷周，据旧以鉴新。其赦天下，与民更始。"

3. 允执厥中：允，诚信。《书·大禹谟》："人心惟危，道心惟微，惟精惟一，允执厥中。" 亦作"允执其中"。《论语·尧曰》："咨！尔舜，天之历数在尔躬，允执其中。"

4. 夙夜在公：从早到晚，勤于公务。《诗·召南·采蘩》："被之僮僮，夙夜在公。"

5. 择善：选择其中好的依从他。《论语·述而》："三人行，必有我师焉，择其善者而从之。"

6. 思齐：看到德才兼备的人，就想向他学习，和他一样。《论语·里仁》："子曰：'见贤思齐焉，见不贤而内自省也。'"

7. 一以贯之：一种思想或理论贯通始终。《论语·里仁》："吾道一以贯之。"

8. 忠信：忠诚信实。语出《论语·公冶长》："子曰：'十室之邑，必有忠信如丘者焉，不如丘之好学也。'"

9. 孝悌：孝顺父母，敬爱兄长。《论语·学而》："其为人也孝弟，而好犯上者鲜矣。"

10. 务本：致力于根本。《论语·学而》："君子务本，本立而道生。孝弟也者，其为仁之本与？"

11. 流谦：《易·象传上·谦》："天道亏盈而益谦，地道变盈而流谦。"

12. 处顺：顺应变化，顺从自然。《庄子·大宗师》："且夫得者时也，失者顺也，安时而处顺，哀乐不能入也。"

13. 北辰：北极星。《论语·为政》："子曰：'为政以德，譬如北辰，居其所而众星共之。'"

14. 一苇能杭：《诗·卫风·河广》："谁谓河广，一苇杭之。"

15. 岁不我与：时光不等人。《论语·阳货》："日月逝矣，岁不我与。"

16. 亲仁善邻：与仁者亲近，与邻邦友好。《左传·隐公六年》："亲仁善邻，国之宝也。"

17. 穆穆在堂：穆穆，端庄恭敬。《书·舜典》："宾于四门，四门穆穆。"宋·郊庙朝会歌辞《歆安之曲》："穆穆在堂，肃肃在庭。"

18. 旧邦新命：《诗·大雅·文王》："周虽旧邦，其命维新。"

19. 功崇业广：取得伟大的功业，是由于有伟大的志向；完成伟大的功业，在于辛勤不懈地工作。《书·周官》："功崇惟志，业广惟勤。"

◎ 译文

公元 2023 年 9 月 28 日，农历癸卯年仲秋时节，至圣先师孔子诞辰 2574 周年，华夏贤达、来自四海的宾朋、孔子后裔，恭敬地用鲜花雅乐敬献于曲阜孔庙大成殿前，庄重纪念孔子、历代的思想家。祭文是：

中华大地多么辽阔！太古混沌初开的年代，日月共同照耀，星辰布满太空。万物共同生长而不互相妨害，万事各依规律运行而不互相冲突。三皇五帝和百姓一道去旧立新。远古帝王忠实地执行正确的原则，周文王、周武王、周成王、周康王从早到晚，勤于公务。

孔子多么有智慧！尼山高耸，洙水畅达，孔子诞生，呈现吉祥。孔子看到德才兼备的人，就向他学习。君子有自己的道德准则和处世方法。用"仁"这一个中心思想贯穿所有的知识。教授《诗经》《尚书》，使六艺传播更加显著。从学生的实际出发，有的放矢地教学，孔子的教育之道宽广浩荡。

孔子多么伟大！忠诚信实，秉持孝悌之道。与人相处，温和亲切，自制谦让。致力于根本的道理，心胸光明开朗。用礼、用音乐陶养人格。提出大同社会和小康生活的政治理想。四季运行，万物由此生长，谦虚顺应，文脉悠久远长。学问经世致用，内具圣人之德，外施王者之政。就像北极星，历经长久的时光依然光明。

神州大地多么雄壮！世界正处于前所未有的大变局，声势浩大，五洲四海都为之激荡。谁说黄河宽广，一苇舟筏就能渡航。时光不等人，前途光明美好。坚持守正创新，自信自强，与各国友好合作，构建人类命运共同体。

中国的儒学是多么繁盛！

中华文明，源远流长。传统文化传承更新，发展繁荣。推动中华优秀传统文化创造性转化和创新性发展，两个结合为努力创造属于我们这个时代的新文化指明方向。文化和文明就在这里，在新时代谱写华章。

今天我们在这里严肃庄重地举行祭祀，就好像孔子仍然在这里。钟鼓声声，琴瑟响亮，孔子思想和祭孔乐曲响彻四方。孔子品格高尚令人仰慕，他的思想令人追求向往。香气氤氲满庭，大成殿肃穆端庄。

拥有伟大的志向，完成伟大的功业。中国式现代化是中华民族的旧邦新命，必将推动中华文明重焕荣光。

我们诚敬而严肃地奉献供品，伏请您享用！

祭孔大典现场　　　　　（图片由济宁日报社提供）

The scene of Confucius Commemoration Ceremony.

Text of the Guimao Year (2023) Confucius Commemoration Ceremony

Written by: Wang Jie

On the Gregorian Calendar, today is September 28, 2023. On the Chinese Lunar Calendar, it is the middle of autumn in the Year of the Water Rabbit. Two thousand, five hundred and seventy-four years have passed since the birth of our master. In honor of the light which he brought to the world, his descendants and friends from all over the world are gathered here today at the Qufu Confucius Temple to experience the scene of the Laying Out Offerings Ceremony, the Rite of Imperial Music, and the Sixty-Four Dancers as we respectfully pay tribute to our ancestor Confucius, the Four Correlates, and other sages. As it is written:

Great China!
The eternal flow of the Yangtze River nurtures everything in accordance with nature.
The people and our gods are all lit by the sun, moon, and stars above.
Emulating the great kings and working from dawn to dusk, fair and righteous behavior is rewarded with civil and military success.
Holy Sage!
This sacred and beautiful land is the master's birthplace at the foot of an auspicious mountain.
Thinking carefully and consistently, a noble person knows the importance of choosing the virtuous path.

Ancient philosophy and ritual are as bright as the north polar star.

Great Master!

Loyalty, filial piety, magnanimity, good etiquette, harmony and prosperity.

To everything there is a season. All things grow and prosper throughout the long ages of mankind.

Wise rulership of the heavens and the earth is apparent to all who look upon it.

Magnificent China!

Unprecedented changes and turbulent times are seen throughout the whole world.

Who says the Yellow River is wide? With determination, even a reed raft can cross it. Time flies by quickly and the road ahead is bright.

Continue to innovate on the basis of practice. Confidence, self-reliance, and kindness to neighbors will lead to harmony for all parties.

Confucianism is great!

Many decades have passed by but word and thought still remain, tied together with fate, and my expectations for greatness remain unabated.

Chinese civilization's strong spirit is born from its long history.

Great things trace their origins to Confucianism and excellence in thought and deed lead to prosperity.

Respect the Master!

The bells ring. The drums beat. The harp strums. The zither resonates. The sounds of celebration are heard in all directions.

Imposing wisdom as weighty as a mountain, academies are filled with learners seeking to know more.

Old lands are meritoriously giving birth to a new destiny. Bless our land with prosperity for all eternity.

I respectfully invite you to make your offerings with solemn piety.

王杰简介

　　王　杰：哲学博士、历史学博士后，中央党校（国家行政学院）教授、博士生导师；中国实学研究会会长，领导干部学国学组委会主任，尼山世界儒学中心理事，全国儒学社团联席会议秘书长，中华母亲节促进会副会长；中宣部核心价值观百场讲坛宣讲人之一；中央电视台"百家讲坛"特别节目《平"语"近人——习近平总书记用典》思想解读嘉宾之一。

　　主要著作：专著《中国哲学十八讲》《先秦儒家政治思想论稿》，主编《领导干部国学大讲堂》《领导干部国学公开课》《领导干部政德公开课》《实学文化丛书》等，在《学习时报》《中国纪检监察报》《人民政协报》《中国领导科学》和中华书局《月读》开设若干学术专栏。

Introduction to Wang Jie

Wang Jie is a Doctor of Philosophy with a postdoctoral degree in History. Professor and doctoral supervisor at the Central Party School (National School of Administration); President of Chinese Society of Shixue, Director of the Organizing Committee for Leading Cadres to Study Chinese Studies, Director of the Nishan World Confucianism Center, Secretary-General of the National Joint Conference of Confucian Societies, Vice President of the Chinese Mother's Day Promotion Association; Presenter at the Publicity Department of the Central Committee of the Communist Party of China's Hundred Forums on Core Values; and Guest Speaker for CCTV's special program series on interpreting the ideology of General Secretary Xi Jinping. His representative works include "Eighteen Lectures on Chinese Philosophy, "and "Discussing Pre-Qin Confucian Political Thought, "and editing "Lectures for Leading Cadres on Chinese Studies, " "Coursework for Officials on Chinese Studies," "Political Ethics for Officials," and "Practical Culture Series." He is the editor-in-chief for Study Times, China Discipline Inspection and Supervision News, Renmin Zhengxie Bao, China Leadership Science, and also a featured columnist for Chung Hwa Book Company's Monthly Digest.

后　记

　　"祭如在，祭神如神在"，祭夫子如夫子在。

　　自 2004 年恢复公祭孔子以来，每年 9 月 28 日均在曲阜孔庙举办隆重的祭孔大典。作为单位的主要职责，济宁市文化传承发展中心（市孔子文化节事务中心）组织筹备了历年的祭孔活动。祭文作为祭孔大典的核心与灵魂，得到了现场嘉宾和儒学界的关注和青睐。每次祭孔活动结束后，祭文印制品均被参祭嘉宾视作珍贵的纪念带回收藏。更多未能现场参祭的专家学者和传统文化爱好者，通过各种渠道索要祭文电子版或在网上检索下载，以供学习研究收藏之用。我有幸担任癸卯（2023）年祭孔大典筹备工作牵头负责人，全程参与其中。祭文的丰富内涵、时代价值、历史意义对现场嘉宾和广大文化爱好者具有极强的吸引力，对此，我感受颇深。

　　至 2023 年，公祭孔子大典已连续举办 20 年。在 2024 年即将迎来孔子诞辰 2575 年之际，将 20 篇祭文汇集成册，感觉很有必要，也是一份沉甸甸的责任，虽然需要克服一些困难。《夫子如在》将祭文进行注释翻译，以飨读者，进而助推讲好中国文化故事济宁篇章，为中华文化发展繁荣尽绵薄之力。

本书的编纂得到了市委领导和市委宣传部的大力支持，市委常委、宣传部部长董冰亲自担任编委会主任，市委宣传部分管日常工作的副部长曹广担任编委会副主任。本书在策划和编纂过程中得到了多位专家的鼎力支持，中央党校教授王杰、山东大学教授杨朝明、曲阜师范大学教授宋立林等专家，充分肯定了本书的意义，并就文体、章节、内容等方面给予了具体指导。杨朝明教授欣然为本书作序。曲阜师范大学孔子文化研究院院长王钧林教授担任主审，整体提升了本书质量。美籍翻译 Marian Deborah Rosenberg 进行了高效准确的英译。济宁日报社刘项清等同志为本书提供了精彩的照片。

市文化传承发展中心全体同志参与了该书的编纂工作。华治、赵相恩、杜忠海三位副主任分工协作、积极推进。王永军、韩开、高保庭、展威等部室负责同志各司其职、认真负责。韩开兼任执行主编，统筹篇章规划，协调编纂工作。靳展、孔冉、李锡楠等编辑人员，承担注释、现代文翻译和校对工作。李巍然、李宁馨等承担部分英文翻译、校对和资料整理工作。全体同志在处理日常繁忙事务的同时，齐心协力，加班加点，历时5个月共同完成了本书稿的编纂工作。

对领导、专家的关心支持和同志们的辛勤付出，在此一并表示感谢。

本书在编纂过程中，力求做到注释准确、语言流畅，英文翻译用词和表达规范，使之成为一部经典荟萃、可读易懂的祷祝文献。由于时间仓促，编者水平有限，难以完全呈现祭文作者的造诣和匠心，书中难免存在疏漏舛误之处，敬请广大读者批评指正。

　　谨以此书向孔子诞辰 2575 年献礼！

　　　　　　　　　济宁市文化传承发展中心主任

　　　　　　　　　2024 年 3 月 26 日

Postcript

"Commemorating as if the Master seems to be present."

In 2004, the Confucius Commemoration Ceremony in Qufu Confucius Temple resumed and since then has been held on September 28th annually. As a major duty, Jining Municipal Cultural Heritage and Development Center, with another name of Jining Municipal International Confucius Culture Festival Affairs Center, has comprehensively organized and hosted the Confucius Commemoration Ceremony over the decades. As the core and essence, the Texts of Commemoration have attracted the attention and favor of guests and researchers of Confucianism. After each Confucius Commemoration Ceremony, the printouts of the commemoration text are cherished and collected by guests as precious souvonir. Furthermore, for those unable to attend the ceremony but still interested in excellent traditional culture, we receive requests for electronic documents of the commemoration texts by any means or attempts to download from the internet for study, research, and collection purposes. As the person in charge of Jining Municipal Cultural Heritage and Development Center, it was my honor to serve as the general coordinator for the Guimao Year (2023) Confucius Commemoration Ceremony and fully participating in the event. The rich content, time value, and historical significance of the commemorial orations have a strong appeal to on-site guests and cultural enthusiasts, leaving a deep impression on me.

By 2023, the Confucius Commemoration Ceremony had been

held continuously for 20 years. In 2024, the 2575th anniversary of Confucius's birth arrives. At this time, it feels necessary and weighty to compile these 20 commemoration texts into a book. Overcoming some difficulties, "Confucius Seems to Be Present" now provides annotations and translations for all readers, thereby promoting the telling of China's cultural stories and Jining's chapters through contributing our efforts to the development and prosperity of Chinese culture.

The compilation of this book received strong support from the CPC Jining Municipal Committee and the Municipal Publicity Department. Dong Bing, Member of the Standing Committee of the CPC Jining Municipal Committee and Minister of Publicity Department, personally served as the director of the editorial board. Cao Guang, Executive Vice Minister of Publicity Department, served as the deputy director of the editorial board. During the planning and compilation process, the book received strong support from several experts, including Professor Wang Jie from the Central Party School, Professor Yang Chaoming from Shandong University, and Professor Song Lilin from Qufu Normal University. They fully recognized the significance of this book and provided specific guidance on style, chapters, content, and other aspects. Professor Yang Chaoming willingly wrote the foreword for this book. Professor Wang Junlin, Dean of the Confucius Culture Research Institute at Qufu Normal University, served as the chief-editor, thereby enhancing the overall quality of the book. The American translator, Marian Deborah Rosenberg, provided efficient and accurate English translations. Mr. Liu Xiangqing from Jining Daily provided wonderful photographs for the book.

All my colleagues from Jining Municipal Cultural Heritage and Development Center participated in the compilation of this book. Vice Directors of our workplace, Hua Zhi, Zhao Xiang'en, and Du

Zhonghai worked together and actively promoted the compilation process. Section Chiefs Wang Yongjun, Han Kai, Gao Baoting, and Zhan Wei, carried out their respective duties diligently and responsibly. Mr. Han Kai also served as the executive editor, coordinating the planning of chapters and overall compilation work. Editors Jin Zhan, Kong Ran, and Li Xi'nan undertook annotation, modern Chinese translation, and proofreading work. Li Weiran and LI Ningxin were responsible for partial English translation, English proofreading, and data organization work. While handling daily busy affairs, all my colleagues worked overtime and on weekends, spending 5 months together to complete the compilation of this book.

I express my heartfelt gratitude to the leaders for their caring support, to the experts for their diligent efforts, and to all colleagues for their hard work.

During the process of compiling this book, efforts were made to ensure accurate annotations, fluent language, and standard expressions in English translations, making it a classic and easy-to-understand practical reference book. Due to time constraints and the limited abilities of our editors, it was difficult to fully present the achievements and ingenuity of the authors of the commemoration texts. Any shortcomings and deficiencies in the book are subject and open to criticism and correction by readers.

With this book, I offer my own tribute to the 2575th anniversary of Confucius' birth!

Director of Jining Municipal Cultural Inheritance and Development Center

Bai Zhande

March 26th, 2024